IS ADOPTION
FOR YOU?

IS ADOPTION FOR YOU?

The Information You Need to Make the Right Choice

Christine Adamec

Foreword by
Jerri Ann Jenista, M.D.

John Wiley & Sons, Inc.

New York • Chichester • Weinheim • Brisbane • Singapore • Toronto

Library of Congress Cataloging-in-Publication Data

Adamec, Christine A.
    Is adoption for you: the information you need to make the right choice / Christine Adamec.
        p.   cm.
    Includes index.
    ISBN 0-471-18312-1 (pbk. : alk. paper)
    1. Adoption—United States—Handbooks, manuals, etc.   I. Title.
HV875.55.A275   1998
362.73′4′0973—dc21   97-25121

Printed in the United States of America

10 9 8 7 6 5 4 3 2 1

CONTENTS

FOREWORD

Back in 1977, when I first started thinking about adoption, I delayed doing anything about the process. I "knew" that in order to adopt, you had to be married, own a house, and have a good job. When I mentioned adopting, my friends and family reacted with comments such as, "Why would you want to do that? It will change your life," or "You're just starting out, you don't have a permanent position, you're not married—how can you possibly raise a child?"

Two years later, I contacted the only adoption agency in my city that would consider a single person. After an application and orientation meeting, the agency said, "We'll call you." Another two years were wasted before I started looking harder.

After writing to more than a hundred agencies and reading the sparse literature the public library offered, I didn't feel much better. Everything I had thought about adoption seemed true. It looked as if only perfect married couples (and not many of them) were allowed to adopt, and then only after undergoing a rigorous (and lengthy and expensive) screening and waiting process.

Then, working as the head pediatrician on a hospital teaching ward, I took care of a newborn, just adopted from India. Talking to the parents, I discovered an informal parent support group. One thing led to another, and within nine months I was at the airport greeting my first daughter, the world's cutest six-week-old. All of this happened in spite of the fact that I was single, lived in a house with no heat or electricity, had no car, was still in school, and had no real job prospects.

My friends and family were right; adoption changed my life. I didn't know anything about being a parent, and certainly nothing about the problems of single and adoptive parents. The only issues I thought about before adopting were whether I could bond to a child not a newborn (six weeks was *so* old!) and what to name the baby.

Now I have five adopted children. Just about every possible adoption scenario is covered in my family: age from newborn to over five years at arrival; special needs ranging from unsuspected serious diagnoses to major risks that turned out to be easily managed or curable; open adoption; birthparent searches; agency vs. private adoption, high cost vs. subsidized costs; long wait vs. no wait. And nearly twenty years after my first timid inquiries, my first prejudice about adoption dissolved when we added a *boy* to the family.

Twenty years ago, I would never have believed that I would build a house with an elevator to accommodate a child in a wheelchair, that I would spend summers running a camp for families with children adopted transculturally, that I would be eager to meet the birthmother of one of my daughters.

Even my career has changed. I was a university academic pediatrician specializing in research on virus infections in newborns. Now I write dozens of educational articles each year on the medical and psychological issues of adoption. I advise parents, agencies, lawyers, social workers, and physicians.

Reflecting on the past two decades, I realize that although my own ideas about adoption have changed, the real change has been in adoption itself. Only a few years ago, adoption was quite restricted. You applied to an agency and did what they told you. If you were not a perfect "Ken and Barbie" family, there was little hope for a child except through the state welfare system or overseas. The paperwork, costs, and bureaucracy deterred many people from adoption. Singles, older people, and families who already had children were on the fringes, worthy of a story in local newspapers because they were so unusual.

Preparation for adoption was minimal, if it existed. In 1980 the education provided by my agency consisted of a group meeting where two or three happy couples described their recent adjustments to an infant. Life as a multiracial family; possible medical problems; relationships with extended family; dealing with finances, health insurance, legal challenges; psychological problems—these issues were not mentioned. Few books were available. The only adoption magazine focused on the process of application and "happy baby" stories after placement.

Today, adoption topics seem to be everywhere—on the news, in magazines and newspapers, in movies and novels, all over the Internet. Agencies, lawyers, colleges, and parent groups offer pre-adoptive counseling and classes. There are magazines, clinics, physicians, and therapists specializing in adoption issues. We read about famous people adopting children—domestic newborns, older children, those with handicaps or siblings, children from overseas. Successful adopted people are found everywhere—including President Gerald Ford, Olympic champions, and wealthy businesspeople.

Even lawmakers have adoption on their minds in legislation on immigration, paternal rights, adoption registries, tax credits, health insurance, parental leave, and employer-provided perks. Open adoption, disclosing of confidential adoption records, media stories focusing on adoptions or adopted children gone wrong—these are all concepts that in the past were only discussed across the back fence or around the kitchen table.

Adoption has definitely changed. More children (in domestic foster care or overseas) and different children (older, handicapped, exposed prenatally to alcohol or drugs) need families. Birthparents now have more say over where their child will be placed. Different kinds of people (older, single, less financially or socially well off, larger families) realize adoption may be an option.

Adoption subsidies, health insurance, and mandatory disclosure of medical information laws have made the process less expensive and less risky. Changes in adoption legislation and policies have allowed lawyers, facilitators, and nontraditional agencies to place children, often more quickly and with less paperwork. People considering adoption are offered a range of pre-adoption services including counseling about adoption, the kinds of adoptive processes, and the different children available.

If there ever was a time to adopt, it is now. Somewhere out there is the right agency or lawyer for every prospective parent. Age, marital status, income, lifestyle, family size—none of these need be an impediment to adoption. Virtually everyone who is looking to adopt today can succeed and in a relatively short time without financial ruin.

If adoption is so great, then why do you need this book, *Is Adoption For You?* You need it because adoption has changed. Because there are so many options to choose from in every aspect of adoption, prospective parents must think harder about their choices than ever before. When it was hard to adopt and only "perfect" couples were accepted, there was a self-selection process. People like me knew they didn't fit the mold and didn't bother to apply. A call or two was enough to confirm the suspicion that you were too old or too poor (or you would become one or the other before your name came to the top of the list.)

Now if one adoption plan doesn't work, you can go elsewhere until you find the program that will place a child with you. You can also get very far into the process without having to think very hard about your decisions. Despite negative media stories, information "out there" announces to you that adoption is not so difficult anymore. Nearly everyone knows somebody who adopted siblings from Russia or a newborn from the United States.

The new attitude is, "If anyone can adopt, why not you?" Friends and family may suggest or even push adoption as a resolution to all kinds of problems besides childlessness. You may actually find yourself pressured to adopt a child.

Adoption is the right option for many more types of parents and children than we imagined a few decades ago. However, it is not the right choice for everyone. *Is Adoption For You?* is a guide to thinking through the issues. After working through this book, you'll be well prepared for any possible adoption question. If you decide not to adopt, you'll know why and you'll feel comfortable knowing that others have made the same decision. If you decide to adopt, you'll be able to anticipate the areas of concern for your situation. You'll be far more able to identify a program that will place the child you really want.

Think of *Is Adoption For You?* as a road map of the United States. You're living childless in New York and you're not so sure if you want to go to adoption-friendly Minnesota or vacationland Florida. After examining the routes you'll have to travel, the obstacles you'll have to overcome, the time you have, and how much you have to spend, you'll make a choice. Neither choice is right or wrong, just different. When you're finished with this book, you'll never again have to wonder wistfully, Should I have considered adoption? Would my life have been different if I had made the other choice? You'll have thought through the issues, and you'll have a good idea that you made the right choice for you.

—Jerri Ann Jenista, M.D.

ACKNOWLEDGMENTS

The most thanks go to my husband, John Adamec, who provided me with practical advice and plenty of emotional support throughout the course of researching and writing this book.

I would especially like to thank the librarians at the DeGroodt Library in Palm Bay, Florida, who provided me with constant encouragement, help and assistance while I researched this book, particularly reference librarians Marie Faure and Pam Hobson, and Mary Scholtz, chief reference librarian.

Others provided direct information or offered themselves as sounding boards for ideas. Esther Gwinnell, M.D., a psychiatrist in private practice in Portland, Oregon, and associate clinical professor in psychiatry at Oregon Health Sciences, responded to many questions and concerns, and provided much-appreciated helpful and positive advice and information. Joseph Kandel, M.D., a noted neurologist and managing partner at the Neuroscience and Spinal Associates in Naples, Florida, and associate clinical professor at Wright State University School of Medicine, offered important creative suggestions and practical advice.

William Pierce, Ph.D., president of the National Council For Adoption, and a longtime friend of adoption, offered his professional advice and assistance and valuable suggestions.

Special thanks to my friend, Jerri Ann Jenista, M.D., a pediatrician in Ann Arbor, Michigan, an adoptive mother to five children, editor of *Adoption/Medical News*, and a household name to most people in the field of adoption. Dr. Jenista offered invaluable assistance and ideas.

I am also very grateful for the assistance provided by the following people: Vika Andrel, J.D., attorney for Andrel Adoptions in Austin, Texas; Maxine Chalker, M.S.W., director of Adoptions From the Heart, an adoption agency in Ardmore, Pennsylvania; Douglas Donnelly, J.D., an adoption attorney in Santa Barbara, California; Jean Nelson-Erichsen, assistant executive director of Los Niños International Adoption Center in The Woodlands, Texas; AnnaMarie Merrill, editor of *Report on Intercountry Adoption* in Boulder, Colorado; Hope Marindin, director of the National Council for Single

Adoptive Parents in Chevy Chase, Maryland; Mary Ann Scherer, R.N., J.D., an adoption attorney in Fort Lauderdale, Florida; Debra Smith, M.S.W., former executive director of the National Adoption Information Clearinghouse and currently a social worker with Coordinators for Adoption in Richmond, Virginia; C. Michael Snyter, Ph.D., a clinical psychologist who counsels prospective adoptive parents in Glendale, Pennsylvania; and Mary Beth Style, M.S.W. and former vice president of professional practice for the National Council For Adoption.

In addition, I thank the many people I interviewed whose names will go unreported: the adoptive parents, individuals considering adoption, and the people who candidly told me how and why they had considered adoption and had decided against or for it.

Thanks also to my editor, Judith McCarthy, for her very valuable ideas and suggestions.

INTRODUCTION

M aking the decision about whether to adopt will probably be one of the biggest decisions of your life, right up there with whether you should be married, whether you should change careers, and other life-changing issues. Because it is so important, you need to give very serious consideration to learning how adoption *really* is today, compared to how adoption and adopted children (and birthmothers and adoptive parents) are depicted in the media—or to what your aunt or neighbor thinks.

Adoption is a scary word and a very thrilling idea when you're thinking about applying it to your own life. Would adopting a child be a good choice for you? Could you create a happy loving family by adoption—or would you be asking for problems that would be just too tough to handle? And, if you seriously consider adopting, will you have to wait five or ten years to adopt, spend every cent you have, and go into serious debt? Can you cope with adoption agencies and probing social workers—what in the world will they ask you and why? What if you don't even get approved after all that work and time and money? And can you live with the common fear that the birthmother will change her mind and your heart will be broken?

On the other hand, the idea of parenting children, watching them grow up, showing them off, or maybe playing ball in the backyard or going on picnics together as a family—or whatever images that you have of yourself as a parent with a child—these and many other special times represent happy moments that you can look forward to if you decide adoption is right for your family.

For many people, adoption is the right answer and will enable them to create the family they have longed for. Over 60,000 infants and older children are adopted by nonrelatives each year in the United States, forming happy families nationwide.

For others, adoption does not really work. Children deserve fully committed parents, and often one spouse is eager to adopt and the other is reluctant. *Is Adoption For You?* covers this issue and discusses ways to work it through. "It's okay to not want to adopt," says Mary Beth Style, M.S.W. and former vice president of professional practice for the National Council For Adoption in Washington, D.C. "Some people think they're supposed to have children, and if they can't have them biologically, then they're supposed to adopt. But adoption is not for everybody."

Many people who have fears and concerns based on inadequate information could be very happy adopting, once they learn the way adoption works and evaluate how they really feel. In order to decide whether you want to become an adoptive parent, you must first decide whether you want to become a *parent*.

Some reasons for parenthood (or for not becoming a parent or an adoptive parent) may surprise you. For example, some people, after studying their lifestyle, their future goals, and the types of people they are, opt for a life without children. Others want children but find they have a variety of reasons for not wanting to adopt. Still others decide to adopt, accepting the joys and challenges of adoptive parenthood.

It's also important to keep in mind that the decision to adopt or not adopt is based on many issues. For example, should you adopt a child of another race? Should you adopt a baby or an older child? What about adopting a child from another country? The kind of child that you envision directly affects your decision for or against adoption.

Good information is essential! Linda is still angry with a state social worker who told her that she could not adopt a baby. The social worker said that it was too hard and instead urged her to apply to adopt a foster child. Eight years later (and still with no child placed in her family), Linda decided to investigate adopting an infant. Within a year, she succeeded. The lesson is that you should not rely on what one person—or even one book—tells you.

Linda said to me, "Don't let social workers or friends (or anyone) talk you into a type of adoption that you're not comfortable with. Don't 'settle' for international or special needs adoption if in your heart you really want to adopt an American newborn of your own race. There is absolutely nothing wrong or selfish about this."

Another issue that concerns some people when trying to decide whether to adopt is adoption fees. Perhaps you think that only rich people or movie stars can adopt children. Not true. One exciting new development in the United States has been the federal tax break of a $5,000 adoption income tax credit. This credit is applied against taxes you owe; for example, if your federal income taxes were $6,000 and your adoption expenses were $5,000 or more, then your tax would be reduced to $1,000. President Clinton signed this legislation into law in 1996 and it became effective in 1997. This change should help many adoptive parents to be able to afford adoption expenses. Contact the IRS for more information.

If you are thinking about adopting an older child (a child who is not an infant or a toddler), there are other issues to consider. For example, the child may have been abused. In any case, the older child comes to you with a history not to be ignored.

It's also important to consider the child's impact on *you*. Whether an infant or an adolescent, this child will continue to affect you and interact in your life with your spouse, family, friends, and others for many years to come. In addition, there is a dynamic interaction *between* you and your child and you will affect each other differently at different points over time. A child's behavior or actions can upset, elate, or desolate you. Your actions can affect the child the same way. Parenthood is not easy.

Other books on adopting tell you how to adopt or how to parent your child after you have adopted. The how-to-adopt books assume that you already know that you want to adopt a child, and they provide the advice and information you need to steer you toward that goal. I have written such a book, *There ARE Babies to Adopt*, and updated it several times. *Is Adoption For You?* is different because it does not assume that you plan to adopt and I believed, based on numerous encounters with people unsure if adoption was for them, that such a book was needed. So I wrote it. I assume that you aren't entirely sure if adopting a child would be the right course to follow and that you are seeking information and advice to help you decide.

Why am I qualified to help you make this important decision? I am both an adoptive parent and a biological parent, so I have parented both ways. I am also the author of seven books, including several on adoption. *The Encyclopedia of Adoption*, written with William Pierce, Ph.D., was a reference book of A–Z essays on adoption. I have also written other how-to books and hundreds of magazine articles on adoption and other topics.

With pediatrician Jerri Ann Jenista, M.D., as my editor, I publish *Adoption/Medical News*, a newsletter that covers a wide variety of medical issues related to adoption.

I am also an adoption advocate, and at the same time, I readily acknowledge that adoption is not a perfect institution and is not right for every person.

DECISIONS TO MAKE

It's a good idea to begin thinking about key issues well before you apply to an adoption agency or attorney. (If you have already applied, however, this book includes practical and usable advice to help you from that point on.) To help you do this, I cover a broad array of issues that look at adoption as a whole and also enable you to look at your personal needs and goals.

Is Adoption For You? will help you work through the myriad questions you have about adoption by providing you with facts about the process and discussing the emotional issues involved. As part of my research, I used clinical studies, articles and books and also performed online research on CompuServe and the Internet. But I have also interviewed real people who have chosen to adopt, as well as people who seriously considered adoption and decided against it. They have been where you are now and have already made their choices, and I believe there is much to learn from them.

If you decide that adoption is right for your family, here are some of the key issues to consider *before* you adopt. (For further information on the issues, be sure to read specific chapters in this book.)

- Should I adopt an infant or an older child?
- Should I adopt through an agency or attorney? In some states, non-agency adoption is unlawful: Massachusetts, Connecticut, and Delaware all ban independent adoption. However, it is still possible to identify a birthmother whose child you would like to adopt and ask an adoption agency to assist you with the adoption.
- Should I adopt from the United States or from another country? If another country, which country?
- If I adopt a baby in the United States, should I agree to involvement and "openness" with the birthmother?

- Am I willing to adopt a child with medical problems? Must these be correctable problems or can I accept long-term or even life-long problems?
- Should I adopt a child of another race or of a mixed race? (If you adopt a child from another country, in many cases you have already answered the race question with a yes.)

Is Adoption For You? also provides you with criteria to look at yourself as a possible future parent. One way to achieve that is to help you see all aspects of yourself. Many people wrongly believe that in order to adopt, you must be a perfect person who has never made a mistake. If that were true, then no one would adopt children!

HOW TO USE THIS BOOK

Is Adoption For You? is divided into four parts. Part One, Understanding the Basics about Adoption, is important because before you can begin evaluating whether adoption might be right for you, you need to take a hard look at existing adoption myths vs. adoption realities. These myths may be holding you or your partner back from adoption. You also need to consider common adoption fears, such as Will the birthmother change her mind about adoption? For this reason, I am including a chart for you on types of birthmothers who are least likely or most likely to change their minds. This information is based on research as well as observations I have made and reported on in the past.

Part One also presents facts about adoption, such as which parents place children for adoption and which children are adopted, as well as what organizations oversee adoption.

Without the general and very important data provided in Part One, you are "flying blind" and cannot make an educated decision. On the other hand, once you have some basic information, then you can far better consider your own circumstances and whether an adopted child would fit into your life.

Part Two enables you to take a look at yourself and compare your personal needs to your potential parenthood and what you can bring to it—and what parenthood would offer to you. Can you "bond" to an adopted child? This is only one of the issues covered in this section. I also include a Self-Evaluation Questionnaire to help you consider yourself and how you might fare as a parent. Another critical area is what your spouse thinks about adoption; many times, spouses don't agree. So what do you do then? This book offers you some ideas to try.

After you consider basic information and take a serious look at yourself, you may still be somewhat unsure. Part Three talks about the questions you may need to ask others. I include a chapter on whether you should consider counseling and how to find a counselor. Another good idea is to network, to capture information you need from the many people and organizations out there: adoptive parent groups, online services, and other opportunities. These topics and more are all covered in Part Three.

Part Four concentrates on unique aspects of adoption that require consideration on their own merits. For example, major differences exist between adopting a child from the United States and adopting one from another country, and this section compares and contrasts the relative advantages and disadvantages. You may also wish to consider a child of another race; transracial adoption is a controversial issue today and one I cover in depth. The chapter also provides comments and suggestions from both non-adopters and adopters who I interviewed.

The Appendix includes important organizations, recommended books, and other resources. I have also included some "bad" and contrasting "good" reasons to adopt.

PART ONE

UNDERSTANDING THE BASICS ABOUT ADOPTION

1

ADOPTION REALITIES VS. MYTHS, FEARS, AND COMMON EMOTIONS

Y ou are thinking about adopting a child but don't know if it's the right decision for you. You have heard plenty of stories and have watched the evening news, and you're worried about whether adoption is really safe or just a road to heartbreak. What you need is information.

WHAT ARE ADOPTIVE PARENTS LIKE?

One way to consider whether adoption would work for your family is to take a look at the people who have adopted already and make some comparisons between them and you. Who are they? What are they like? Are they like you?

Although many adoptive parents are single, the majority are married couples. (Chapter 8 covers single parent adoption.) Most people who adopt undergo a screening process known as a home study, which is a background investigation of the prospective adoptive parents and much more than a visit or two to the home. Increasing numbers of agencies and attorneys are also requiring applicants to undergo psychological testing and evaluation as well. As a result, most people who ultimately become adoptive parents are stable and healthy individuals.

Many adoptive parents have a better track record at marriage than parents who never adopted a child (possibly because people who have been married numerous times have been turned down by adoption agencies). Many adopt only one child and thus become one-child families, but some go on to adopt more children. Others already have biological children or give birth to children after adoption. Contrary to popular myth, however, only about 6 to 7 percent of adoptive parents give birth after adopting, according to a study by Michael Bohman in *Adopted Children and Their Families*.

Adoptive parents are generally well educated, with at least a high school diploma. One 1990 government study indicated that only about 7 percent of adoptive parents did not have a high school education. About half of all adoptive parents have a four-year college degree and some have graduate degrees.

Careerwise, adoptive parents are typically in middle-class career fields. Many adoptive parents are in their mid to late thirties when they adopt, although as the baby boomers age, upper limits appear to be increasing. About ten years ago, many agencies would not accept applicants who were over age forty; now many more will accept them as applicants or let birthmothers decide if they want older parents for their child.

When it comes to international adoption, anecdotally I would say that parents may be a little older still, in their late thirties or forties when they adopt; however, some countries will allow people in their fifties to adopt because the need for families is so great in their countries.

Most adoptive parents are healthy, but this does not mean they have no health problems. It means that they have the capacity to parent actively now and until the child is at least eighteen years old. Some disabled people adopt children when they can meet a child's needs. Many adoptive parents are infertile, with either a primary infertility (they have never had children) or secondary infertility (they have had children but cannot have more).

TEN ADOPTION MYTHS

General myths about adoption and specific myths about people involved in the adoption process have always existed. For example, many myths are associated with birthmothers: that they nearly always want their babies back or that they are either bad or saintly. A primary myth is that most adopted children and adults are disturbed people. But probably the most prevalent myth of all is that it is not possible to adopt, so I will address this one first.

Myth #1: Adoption Is Impossible

It is possible to adopt a baby or older child today, despite what is conveyed to you in the media or through conversations. According to the myth, millions of people are actively competing to adopt a child. This assumption usually is based on statistics of the total number of people seeking help at fertility clinics. The reality is that about half of the people who go to physicians for help with conception do eventually succeed in achieving a pregnancy and consequently will never attempt to adopt a child.

Of those who cannot conceive or who cannot carry a baby to term, not all wish to adopt. Keep this critical point in mind: Many people (and you may be one of them) will decide against adoption. Maybe they believe that they would be happy only with a biological child. (Note: "biological" is a term used in adoption to connote children born to a family.) Others do not wish to deal with the bureaucracy (or what they perceive as the bureaucracy) involved in adopting or to pay the adoption fees. Or they have myriad other reasons (many of which are discussed throughout this book) for why they decide against adoption.

Myth #2: Birthmothers Are Bad Girls

The second most prevalent myth is that the biological mother wants her child adopted because she doesn't really care about it and just wants to get rid of it. She is often, according to this myth, a promiscuous drug user who probably has AIDS.

"I feel that there still can be a lot of punitiveness, even among doctors or nurses—like you [the birthmother] committed a sin and you're going to have to pay for it. I've seen nurses refuse to bring painkillers to birthmothers—their personal feelings really override their professionalism," says Vika Andrel, attorney for Andrel Adoptions in Austin, Texas. "It's not because they're bad people that they are choosing adoption. Maybe they're living in a bad situation."

The reality is that birthmothers are typically working-class or middle-class people. Most do not have AIDS or a drug problem.

Most are not on welfare. Most do not have a steady stream of sexual partners.

Often, a woman who chooses to place her child for adoption had what to her was a meaningful relationship with a man. Maybe she thought the man would marry her, or maybe she wanted a long-term live-in lover. In any case, she responded to what she thought was love. Then she became pregnant.

Pregnant women who choose adoption generally do not want to go on public assistance, even for a few months. They want to be independent and they are thinking about their future and the future of the child. For personal, health, or religious reasons, they don't choose abortion. Or perhaps they've delayed the decision too long for the procedure to be done safely or legally in their state.

As a result, a pregnant woman may see adoption as the logical and loving answer. She knows that many people want to adopt children. She knows (or can quickly find out) that the family who adopts her child will be financially secure and will be screened by an agency or independent social worker.

The birthmother who chooses adoption under today's circumstances is usually a very brave and strong-willed person, one who can and does buck the trend toward today's highly accepted single parenting.

But this leads us to another (and, admittedly, rarer) myth about birthmothers—that they are so good, so pure to make this unimaginable decision that they must be saintly.

Myth #3: Birthmothers Are Saints

Perhaps this myth has arisen in an overreaction to the "bad girl" birthmother myth. Some people, primarily those who are adopting or have adopted, as well as some adoption professionals, put the birthmother high up on a pedestal. They believe that the birthmother who chooses adoption for her child is so self-sacrificing that she must be elevated to sainthood. She is one in a million, she is one who places her child's needs before her own needs. She is so perfect that she is even better than the adoptive parents (and a lot of other people, too).

Except, of course, she isn't a saint. She is a pregnant woman who is considering both her child's needs and her own, and she has concluded that parenthood is not a feasible choice for her now. She doesn't want to "give away" or "throw away" her baby, but neither is she a perfect person.

Instead, birthparents choosing adoption are unready to be parents and they know it, but they want the child to have a good and loving family. This is difficult for many infertile people to accept. But I think that unless and until you can comprehend that a birthmother is just another human being—one who is just as normal or flawed or fallible as you are—you need to continue thinking about, rather than acting on, adopting a child.

Myth #4: Birthparents Always Want Their Babies Back

"I think a paramount fear of adoptive parents is whether this is going to be a permanent thing, whether there are going to be any challenges after the adoption is finalized," says Mary Ann Scherer, a Fort Lauderdale, Florida, attorney who has facilitated more than a thousand adoptions. "The media focus on the negative aspects of adoption clouds the positive results in adoptive placements, and adoptive parents don't realize that 98 percent of the adoptive placements are working fine."

Most readers will be well aware of cases such as "Baby Jessica" in Michigan and "Baby Richard" in Illinois, in which birthparents successfully fought legal battles to obtain custody of their children. In these cases, the children were three years old before they were sent to the biological parents. The heartrending scenes of hysterical children being separated from their adoptive parents upset many people nationwide—adoptive parents or not.

As a direct result of such scenes, many people mistakenly assume that it is now dangerous to adopt a baby in the United States. They think that after a few months or years, the birthparents will decide they want the child back. Instead, the reality is that twenty-five thousand to thirty thousand babies in the United States and eleven thousand children from other countries (most of whom are infants) are adopted each year. No trumpets, no fanfare—except in the hearts and minds of the adoptive parents and their extended families.

Understandably, many people make a hasty generalization and think that if one highly publicized adoption went sour, all adoptions must be at risk. This is patently untrue.

It's also important to keep in mind that each state has its own laws on adoption and they vary radically. Some obtain the consent for adoption from a birthparent within days of the birth, and it is irrevocable—no change of mind allowed. Other states allow weeks or months for a change of heart to occur.

Because so many people are worried about birthparents who change their mind about placing a child for adoption, even after making elaborate arrangements, I've created a chart for you. A teaching tool I have used before, the chart is based on my interviews with experts over a decade, my observations, and numerous scientific studies. This chart indicates types of birthmothers who are least likely and most likely to change their minds about the adoption plan. Keep in mind that a birthmother who fits my profile may act differently; for example, a high school graduate may change her mind about adoption while a high school dropout carries through her plan. Also, most birthmothers do not fit *all* of this criteria. In general, however, this is a good tool.

Whether the adoption will be confidential or some information will be disclosed between adoptive parents and birthparents, I recommend that adopting parents consider the following patterns among women considering adoption for their babies.

Birthmother Least Likely to Change Mind	*Birthmother Most Likely to Change Mind*
High school graduate	High school dropout
Lives in rural area	Lives in city
Her own mother approves of adoption	Mom disapproves of or does not know about plan
Lives away from parents	Lives with parents
Has no relationship with the baby's birthfather	Has continuing relationship with the baby's birthfather
Is religious	Not religious
Has plans for after child's birth (college, career, etc.)	Has no plans for future
Is not on public assistance (welfare)	Is on welfare (The longer she has been on public assistance, the higher the probability that she will change her mind)
Her parents have more than a high school education	Her parents have high school education or less
Raised in two-parent family	Raised by single parent

Seeks minimal contact with infant after birth	Seeks continuous contact with infant directly after birth (This does not refer to open adoptions.)
Not living in permanent home	Living in permanent home where she'll stay after birth of child
Not dependent on same income source as the baby's birthfather	She and the baby's birthfather rely on same income

Myth #5: Most Adopted Children Are Disturbed

Some people still believe that adopted children are more likely to ex-perience serious psychological or medical problems than non-adopted children. Certainly, if you adopt an older child who was abused, neglected, or abandoned, you need to be prepared to deal with any psychological problems that child may have as a result of this mistreatment. But most people adopted as infants grow up to be healthy and happy.

Many studies support this. Probably the best is a study of 881 adopted teenagers, accomplished by the Search Institute in Min-neapolis, Minnesota. The findings, published in 1994, revealed that in most cases, adopted teenagers were as well adjusted as the non-adopted kids. (The children had all been adopted as babies.) So the image of the unhappy, mixed-up adopted child as the standard really doesn't hold up.

In another study that compared the adjustment levels of three groups of children—those being raised by single biological parents, those raised by adoptive parents, and those raised by two-parent bio-logical families—the adopted children fared much better than the children being parented by single birthparents, and in most categories, they fared as well as the biological children raised in a two-parent family.

And a range of studies of Korean-born adopted children, re-ported by Wun Jung Kim, M.D., in his 1995 article in *Child Psychi-atry and Human Development*, found that Korean children have shown an amazing level of adaptability and resilience. Indeed, in some cases these children have achieved at higher levels than white or black adopted children.

Dr. Kim provides study after study revealing that the majority—as many as 80 percent—of children adopted from Korea are doing quite well in the United States. (For more information on international adoption, see Chapter 13.)

Some adopted children do have emotional or psychological problems, particularly if they were adopted as older children. This is generally why some studies indicate higher populations of adopted children in clinical studies of emotionally disturbed children—they include children who were adopted *as* older children.

Also, children who have been living in orphanages and receiving very little nurturing (and in some cases, little medical care, education, and other attention that Americans take for granted) often will suffer and show the effects of this suffering. Yet it's also important to realize that even if you adopt a healthy newborn who is two days old, that child could possibly develop problems later on in life. Whether your child is born to you or adopted by you, children come with no guarantees. Adoption agencies don't issue warranties on children.

Myth #6: Adoptive Parents Aren't as Good as Biological Parents—They're "Second Best"

Few adoptive parents like to think about this, but some people in our society believe that adopting a child is a last resort and is not as good as parenting a child who was born to you. "I think there is still a perception that a biological family is a very sacred thing and an adoptive family is sort of like a stepsister who should be in the basement," says attorney Vika Andrel of Andrel Adoptions in Austin, Texas. "People think a biological family is better and isn't it too bad that you couldn't have your 'own' children." Andrel says that many people who decide to adopt will encounter this attitude and need to learn how to deal with it.

You should feel that adoption is not a second-class option, while at the same time realizing that adoption is not completely the same as birthing a child. Douglas Donnelly, an adoption attorney from Santa Barbara, California, says, "I have a concern if people who pursue adoption think that this will be a total 100% substitute for the biological parenting experience. I say if you're looking for a complete substitute, adoption is not for you. If you can 'settle' for 95 percent of the loaf, then you're going to love adoption. But if that 5 percent that you can't have is going to eat you up, don't pursue adoption."

Of course, most adoptive parents are infertile couples who wanted to create a biological child and were unable to do so. The women wanted to experience what pregnancy was like and to feel a child growing inside them. But when prospective parents make the choice for adoption, the overwhelming majority become strongly committed to that choice and to the children they subsequently adopt.

Some studies indicate not only that adoptive parents are not second-class parents, but they may in fact be *better* parents than biological parents are. A 1995 study reported by Susan Golombok et al. compared and contrasted four groups of parents: parents of children conceived through in vitro fertilization; parents of children conceived through donor insemination; adoptive parents; and biological parents. The groups were matched to be as close as possible in many respects.

Golombok found that the level of quality of parenting in the families with assisted reproduction was higher than that of the biological families. The adoptive families' parenting was also superior to that of the biological parents. Even though the assisted reproduction families included some genetic link and the adoptive parents had no genetic link to their children, few differences were found between the two groups:

> The findings suggest that genetic ties are less important for family functioning than a strong desire for parenthood. Whether the child was genetically unrelated to one parent, [as] in the case of donor insemination, or [the child was] genetically unrelated to both parents, in the case of adoption, the quality of parenting in families where the mother and father had gone to great lengths to become parents was superior to that shown by mothers and fathers who had achieved parenthood in the usual [biological] way.

A study by Rachel Levy-Shiff et al. comparing Israeli biological parents to adoptive parents, published in a 1991 issue of *Developmental Psychology*, found that adoptive parents had a better transition to parenthood than the biological parents. The process did appear different, however, in that social support was important for the adoptive parents and was also a good predictor of their success as parents.

Of course, what is important is how *you* feel about adoption. If you feel that adoption is second-best and if you aren't sure you could feel truly fulfilled or "real" with an adopted child, you should carefully consider these important issues.

Myth #7: Only Rich People Adopt

Although expenses are nearly always incurred when adopting a child, most people who adopt are not upper-class captains of industry or glittering movie stars. Probably because so many believe that only the rich adopt, some people protested the adoption tax credit for healthy children, which was passed by Congress and signed by President Clinton into law in 1996 (effective 1997 through 2001). They wondered out loud why wealthy people needed and should be allowed to have a tax credit for adopting a healthy baby.

Most adoptive parents are middle-class people who must come up with considerable cash to finance the cost of an adoption. An adoption tax credit is a great help to them. Many people adopting a child from the United States or from another country may now take a tax credit of $5,000, and those adopting a U.S. child with special needs, such as medical problems, may take a tax credit of up to $6,000.

The passage of this legislation provided the first broad-based financial relief to adoptive parents in several decades—and may well lead to more people choosing the adoption option.

So how do these middle-class Americans afford adoption fees, which can range from $15,000 to $20,000 or more? They borrow from their families. They tap into their savings and IRAs. They take out loans. They sell belongings.

It's also important to note that increasing numbers of corporations offer adoption benefits to their employees, with an average of about $2,000 per family. This employee benefit is offered by some companies because it is thought to equalize maternity benefits paid to people who have biological children or even medical benefits paid to people who are seeking infertility options such as in vitro fertilization and other choices.

This leads to a question that is frequently asked: Shouldn't adoption be inexpensive or even free, because it is a social good? The problem is that hospitals charge fees for childbirth and adoption agencies have to pay social workers' salaries (and heat, lights, phone bills, etc.). Perhaps adoption fees are too high—but we must deal with the world as it is, not as we would like it to be.

Myth #8: If You Adopt, You'll Get Pregnant

Many people remain convinced that this is true—because they have a friend of a friend who did adopt and did become pregnant. As I mentioned earlier, pregnancy after adoption happens in about 6 to 7 percent of the people who adopt children.

Should women even continue to seek a pregnancy after they adopt? That's a very individual decision. Doreen was quite annoyed when a relative asked her, after the adoption of her daughter, if she and her husband were still "trying." The new adoptive mom said with some irritation, "Well, we still make love sometimes!" (Whether it was the tone or the words used—the message got across and the relative left her alone after that.)

So if a pregnancy can happen, sometimes it does after an adoption. But most adoptive parents do not have a biological child after they adopt. If anyone adopts in order to somehow make a pregnancy and birth magically happen, he or she is making a serious mistake and is being very unfair to the adopted child.

Myth #9: If God Wanted You to Have a Baby, You'd Get Pregnant

I can tell you that I get pretty heated up by this myth, and it's a fairly common one. The assumption is that if you can't have children, there must be *some* reason and maybe it's because God didn't want you to have kids. Or maybe it's because of something you did in the past, something that somehow impaired your fertility and resulted in the problem you now have in conceiving a child. You don't really know *what* it is that you did, but you just know you must be guilty! My belief is that your current infertility is not a divine "punishment" for past actions.

An underlying aspect of this guilt is the belief that you are in control of what happens to your body. Often, this is not true. Countless processes are going on in your body right now as you read this book. Your heart is pumping, your lungs are taking in oxygen, your stomach is digesting, cells are dying and being replaced, chemicals in your brain are reacting, and on and on. Are you consciously in control of those processes?

What you need to realize—and this can be very difficult for some of us to accept—is that sometimes no matter how hard you try to achieve something, it doesn't work.

Whether it's finding the perfect job, attracting the man or woman of your dreams, or creating a pregnancy—despite your best efforts, some goals you've set cannot be reached. But this does not mean it is your fault or that you are evil or guilty in some way.

Another aspect of this "it's your fault" myth that I find disturbing is the presumption that you must not be good enough, otherwise, God would have allowed you to get pregnant. It doesn't make much sense, does it? Would God want all those unmarried teenage girls to have babies rather than you? Few of them are competent parents. I personally believe that God smiles upon adoptive parents, their children, and birthparents, for seeking a good plan for a child.

Myth #10: Adopted Kids Don't Attach to Adoptive Parents

Another common myth is that adopted children really don't become attached to their adoptive parents and other relatives and vice versa. The reality is that in most cases, both children and adults become attached to each other and are a very real family. Many studies, such as the one done by the Search Institute that I mentioned earlier, have shown this to be true.

I can cite my own example. When my adopted son's grandfather died, he was devastated. He was about five years old, and he and Grampa were a devoted team. Steve was used to playing hide-and-seek with Grampa; Grampa always took a long time to find him, even though everyone else heard Steve giggling in his hiding place. Before Grampa died, I took Steve to see him in the hospital, and that poor ill man . . . his eyes lit up like the aurora borealis when he saw my boy, and the affection was returned in kind. For a few moments, he forgot his own pain and experienced joy. There was no genetic link. But there was a strong emotional link. And after his grandfather's death, Steve grieved for him.

COMMON FEARS AND ASSUMPTIONS
ABOUT ADOPTION

Tied in with the myths about adoption are many common fears; some are valid, some are not. We've already discussed the fear of the birthmother changing her mind, but other equally common fears influence the decision to adopt.

With so much media focus on AIDS, many people are afraid to adopt a baby because they fear it may be HIV positive. (HIV refers to the human immunodeficiency virus, which causes AIDS.)

Many people fear that the behavior of the birthmother during pregnancy—predominantly her drug or alcohol use—will harm the child. They may also worry about bonding to a child not born to them, or they may be afraid that they won't know how to be good parents.

Some men and women also fear that they will lose their personal identity as well as their marital identity should they become parents. Some people also fear a loss of privacy. Let's take a look at some of these fears and begin to address them.

Fear of AIDS

Many adoption agencies report that prospective adoptive parents are worried that the child they plan to adopt may be born HIV positive, and thus they want a screening test of the child. (In some cases, children overseas are tested in the orphanage.)

What if the birthmother is tested during pregnancy—isn't that enough? It usually is, because if the HIV virus is there, it will show up in most cases. Another important reason for testing a pregnant woman at risk for HIV (a drug abuser or a woman with many sexual partners) is to protect the fetus. If she tests positive for HIV, she can take a drug called zidovudine (AZT), and this will in many cases prevent the infant from getting AIDS.

For the reason just given, the American Medical Association has recommended that all pregnant women be tested for HIV. As of now, such testing cannot be mandated; however, an adopting parent can certainly request that it be done. Your adoption agency or attorney may already routinely request this testing.

Many babies born in the United States are tested for HIV at birth. You may wonder about the accuracy of these tests. In fact, most children test negative and *are* negative, say pediatricians. Why? Because if the birthmother had HIV, she would produce antibodies in her system and they would show up in the baby, whether the baby had HIV or not. Thus a newborn can test positive even though the baby doesn't have HIV.

False positives to HIV are far more common when the birthmother herself is HIV positive, because of the transfer of maternal antibodies. But only about 25 percent of these babies are infected. Increasingly sophisticated tests are able to determine in a matter of weeks whether the infant actually has HIV.

There are *very few* false negatives—the baby tests negative but actually does have the HIV virus. A false negative in a newborn infant could occur if the mother acquired the HIV infection toward the end of her pregnancy and her own system had not yet converted to HIV positive—a window of about six weeks. In such a case, the baby could test negative because the mother is testing negative.

To summarize, if the newborn tests negative, then she or he is almost surely negative for HIV. If the infant tests positive, she or he may still be uninfected, but further testing is required.

What about older kids? Presuming that the child has not been sexually abused, the child who tests negative for HIV *is* negative. By this time, any antibodies from the biological mother are definitely out of the child's system.

Fears of the Birthmother's Drug and Alcohol Consumption During Pregnancy

Some people are fearful that the birthmother may be an alcoholic or a substance abuser. Or, if their fear does not extend that far, they may worry that the stress of pregnancy could cause her to drink or abuse drugs.

Even if you knew the birthmother, you could not be with her every minute of every day, so you will have to trust and hope that abuse will not occur. Some agencies and attorneys do random testing for drugs and alcohol, and they do receive reports back from the doctor's office. Testing also occurs at the time of the child's birth.

The reason for concern with alcohol abuse is that the child could be born with Fetal Alcohol Syndrome (FAS), a serious problem that causes many neurological difficulties and may also cause retardation in the infant as well as a variety of physical ailments.

FAS is very obvious in some children because of characteristic facial features, small head size, and other traits most doctors are very familiar with. Sometimes the problem is not so evident, however, and may not be readily diagnosable until the infant is older.

In the case of drug abuse, most of us have heard about cocaine babies, those born addicted to crack cocaine and who howl continuously—making the distressing colic that some normal infants suffer from seem like a day at the beach in comparison. The prognosis for cocaine babies is not clear. Longitudinal studies are being done, and it appears that some children are doing well.

A very complicating problem is that it's hard to know what problems, if any, to attribute to the crack use because most cocaine-using mothers also abused alcohol and other substances, probably didn't get much prenatal care, and ignored basic nutritional needs. Despite all of this, the infant may still be okay. Or not. The adoptive parents are the ones who must decide whether it is worth it to take the risk.

Do *not* assume that if you adopt a child from another country, you will be somehow "safe" from the problem of birthmothers who abuse alcohol. Physicians report seeing cases of FAS from several countries of the former Soviet Union.

Fear of Being a Good Parent: Can *You* Do It?

Just about all future parents, whether the child comes through birth or adoption, worry about whether they will be able to be good parents. How can you teach a child all the important moral values unless you are a paragon of virtue yourself? How can you take a small person and help mold him or her into a happy productive adult?

Keep in mind that nobody expects you to be perfect. Or, if they do, they are going to be very disappointed! The key to successful parenting, in my opinion, is to learn as much as you can by reading books and talking to others and then calibrating the advice to the needs of your child. It's also important to remember that it's nearly always possible to rectify the mistakes that you will inevitably make. And if not, you apologize.

COMMON EMOTIONS ASSOCIATED WITH ADOPTION

When you are trying to decide if you should adopt, you are probably running through many of the same emotions experienced by others in your situation. This section describes frequently occurring negative and positive emotions experienced by people trying to make this difficult decision.

Frustration

Both infertility and the adoption process generate plenty of frustration. It's partly a sense of the "unfair" aspect and partly a feeling that you want to *do* something to change it all but you can't figure out what.

Knowledge is power. If you are infertile, the more you know about your fertility problem, the better you will understand your feelings and work toward acceptance. Ask your doctor to explain medical terms to you in plain English. Find out if there is any chance that you can have a biological child—one in ten, one in a thousand, one in a million, none?

It's also frustrating to agonize over whether you should adopt a child. You may turn over every reason for and against and still have trouble deciding. Again, the more you know, the better decision you can make.

Impatience

If you've had years of infertility treatments and now have decided that you want to adopt right away, you may feel well justified in being impatient because you have been waiting so long.

You've heard about incredibly long waiting lists at adoption agencies and may feel as if you can't possibly bear to wait five or more years to adopt. You may even think, Why bother? By then, I'll be too old.

The reality is that in many cases, people can adopt children within a year or two and sometimes faster. If you apply to one agency that has a five-year waiting list, then you'll probably wait five years. But if you seek out an agency or attorney that places many children and has a shorter waiting period or works in intercountry adoptions, then you will probably wait less time.

Sometimes one partner becomes impatient with the other, and wonders aloud why they should spend yet more money on another in vitro fertilization or other treatment, which might not work, when adoption would bring them a child. Often husband and wife are not in sync with each other on when it is time to give up infertility treatments and seek to adopt. In fact, this disparity is so common that some agencies call it the "dragger/draggee" problem (see Chapter 5).

Hopelessness and Futility

Another common emotion among people who are trying to overcome infertility as well as among people who are considering adoption is a feeling that both are hopeless ventures, so why even bother? When you are on your fourth or fifth in vitro fertilization and it doesn't result in a "take home baby" (a term fertility clinics use), it's easy to get discouraged. And maybe, in this case, you should become discouraged. The odds go down after several unfulfilled attempts, and you need to ask your doctor what your actual chances of achieving a pregnancy are.

You may also feel that adoption is an impossible and unachievable dream. You may wonder why you should subject yourself to more emotional pain. You ask yourself, Haven't I suffered enough?

Many people fall into this emotional slump at one time or another. One possible cure is to learn about adoption. The more you find out, the better prepared you are to make the decision for or against this choice. It's also a good idea to meet some adoptive parents. It can be immensely uplifting to walk into a roomful of parents with adopted babies. This is one reason why I recommend adoptive parent groups.

Lack of Control

You may also feel disturbed by your apparent lack of control in the adoption process. You may feel like you are at the mercy of agencies or attorneys who know the system far better than you do. You're right in one aspect—they do know the system. But it is certainly one that can be mastered by most adopting parents. If you have a fear of a lack of control, keep reading!

Euphoria

If you decide to proceed with adoption, most of you will find that the day your child arrives is one filled with a euphoria that is hard to describe—you can't believe it! Your child is finally really really here! The thrill of seeing your child for the first time can send you into the stratosphere with joy. Of course, many new parents need a few days to become used to the idea of parenthood. It's perfectly normal if it takes some time to fall in love with your child.

Relief

Relief is another emotion mentioned by many adoptive parents as well as people who have considered adoption and decided against it. At last! The decision is *made*. For example, Becky said it was a tremendous relief, after seven years, to get away from constant visits to doctors and clinics. "It was wonderful to be done with all that and get on with a more normal life."

Becky found she had to rebuild relationships with others because she had obsessed on fertility treatment for all those years. "We did it differently with adoption," she said. "Infertility is the great silence and we didn't tell anyone. But with adoption, we told our family and friends at work. Adoption was a sure thing and fertility was not. When we decided on adoption, we did everything we could and it was a fast process." She and her husband adopted within a year.

Thankfulness

Some adoptive parents feel that the opportunity to adopt a child was a gift from God. For example, Joe and Lisa adopted three children. "We have a real strong belief in God and we felt like this was part of his plan for us—he was kind of our ultimate social worker," said Joe.

For a while, Lisa was still disappointed about her infertility. She said, "After our second adoption, we sorted out the difference between infertility and adoption and we concluded that although infertility was a disappointment, the child was a far greater issue of importance." She added, "When I was trying to get pregnant, I used to cry every Mother's Day. Not anymore."

2

BASIC FACTS
ABOUT ADOPTION

B efore you can really begin to look at yourself as a prospective adoptive parent, you need a basic grasp of what adoption is—and of what it is not. This chapter provides critical data you need in your decision-making process.

WHAT IS ADOPTION?

Adoption is the complete and permanent transfer of parental rights and obligations, usually from one set of legal parents to adoptive parents. In most cases, the biological parents (also called birthparents, birthmother, or birthfather) freely choose adoption and willingly sign consent forms. When adopting a child from within the United States, it's a good idea to have both the birthmother and the birthfather sign consent forms, whenever possible.

If the birthfather does not wish to sign consent to adoption, it's a good idea for the adoption professional to try to obtain a statement from the birthfather that he is not the father and/or that he does not object to the adoption. This is not always possible, because the birthfather may be unknown (or the birthmother says that he is) or the birthfather cannot be located. In such cases, often the adoption agency or attorney will formally publish notification of the impending adoption in a newspaper.

In some cases, the parental rights of the birthparents are taken away by a judge, usually because the parents have abused, neglected, or abandoned their children and numerous counseling attempts have failed to pull the family back together. Involuntary terminations of parental rights often do not occur until a child has been in foster care for years and the child is at least six or seven years old.

If the child is adopted from another country, she or he is considered an "orphan" by the definitions of the U.S. Immigration and Naturalization Service (INS). Often the child was abandoned at an orphanage.

Nearly always, when parents choose adoption for their children, the children are infants. Very rarely are they toddlers and older. This is important to note, because many people mistakenly believe that it is easier to adopt a two-year-old child than it is to adopt a baby. Instead, the reverse is true (unless you adopt from another country).

Few U.S. birthparents are willing to sign consent to an adoption when their children are two years old or older because by that time they are too attached to them to choose adoption. An exception might be if the mother has a terminal illness and cannot find anyone to care for her children; however, this is not common.

An adoption is "finalized" by a court after a certain period, on average about six months, but each state has its own adoption laws and its own time frame to finalization. When an adoption is finalized in a U.S. court, a new birth certificate is subsequently issued with the adoptive parents' names as the parents and the original birth certificate is "sealed" so that only a court order could release it. It is extremely difficult to overturn a finalized adoption and is seldom done.

WHAT ADOPTION IS NOT

Adoption is not foster parenthood or legal guardianship, although many in the media constantly confuse these concepts with the adoption choice.

A foster parent is usually a person who is licensed by the state or county (and sometimes by a private adoption agency) to provide temporary care to a child who cannot live with his or her parents for some reason. Although some foster parents may care for children for years, in most cases they have no rights in the courtroom over what happens to the child and no legal standing to object if he or she is sent back to formerly abusive parents. This seems very unfair to most foster parents (and to me), but it is the way the program usually works in most states.

Legal guardianship is given to adults who wish to care for a child when a parent cannot provide care. This quasiparental control is usually given by the parent. It is generally considered a temporary state and one that can be ended, at virtually any time and usually by the parent in court.

Some adults have willingly become legal guardians when parents have requested them to do so, presuming that after some time frame, they would be allowed to adopt. But the parents can and frequently do decide that they want custody returned, sometimes after years, and the parents' wishes nearly always prevail. Never assume that legal guardianship can be a fast, easy, and inexpensive way to adopt a child. I have known people who made this mistake and who were brokenhearted later.

WHO PLACES CHILDREN FOR ADOPTION?

Birthmothers may be of any childbearing age, but most are in their late teens or early twenties if they voluntarily choose adoption. This doesn't mean young teens never choose adoption—but they are more likely to catapult back and forth between yes and no and are very susceptible to the influence of others.

Most birthmothers who choose adoption are not married. Birthparents are typically middle-class or working-class people, but not always.

The common denominator, regardless of their social status and income, is that birthparents who choose adoption do not feel ready or able to parent a child.

Biological Fathers

When the birthfather is known, his permission for the adoption is also sought. If the birthfather is married to the birthmother, he is presumed the biological father (whether he is or not), and all states require the husband's permission to the adoption. If another man is the actual genetic father, his permission should be sought as well, although court decisions have been mixed on whether the genetic father's permission is needed when a birthmother is married to another person.

The birthfather may refuse to acknowledge paternity but he may be willing to sign a document that states that he claims he is not the father and has no legal interest in the custody of the infant. Some states allow the birthfather to sign consent even before the child is born.

The psychological ramifications of fatherhood have only recently been recognized. Until about a decade ago, the prevailing assumption was that birthfathers were always relieved when a family adopted the child and took the psychological and financial responsibilities from his shoulders. This is often true; however, in some cases, the birthfather does wish to parent his child and can provide a good home. In some cases, the birthfather's mother wishes to parent the child and presses the birthfather to pursue his paternity and custody claim.

State laws on birthfathers' rights vary radically from state to state. In some states, if the birthfather is not listed with a "birthfather registry," then he cannot claim his paternal rights. In others, the burden of proving that the birthfather is not seeking custody of the child lies with the adoption agency or attorney.

WHO IS ADOPTED?

Shockingly, no government agency tracks the numbers of children who are adopted, but the National Council For Adoption estimates that about fifty thousand children are adopted each year within the United States by nonrelatives. About twenty-five thousand to thirty thousand of these children are infants.

In addition, Americans adopt about eleven thousand children from other countries, and most are infants or small children. The Immigration and Naturalization Service oversees international adoption and does collect data.

Children who are adopted may be just a few days old or they may be any age up to eighteen years.

Adopted children may be of any race and may be of mixed races and ethnic backgrounds. They may be completely healthy or profoundly disabled, physically or emotionally, and it's important for adoptive parents to consider ahead of time what, if any, disabilities or differences they feel they can deal with (see Chapter 15).

THE ADOPTION PROFESSIONALS

Another key player in the adoption placement drama is the adoption agency or adoption attorney. Most adoptions are facilitated through social workers employed at private adoption agencies or through attorneys.

State Agencies

Each state has a state social services department that oversees the foster care program and that places foster children for adoption. Many of the foster children who need adoptive families are well over age five or six and many have been abused, neglected, or abandoned. Some are infants with severe medical problems. However, state agencies place very few infants who do not have special needs.

Private Adoption Agencies

Private adoption agencies are licensed by the state. Most place infants, but some place older children. Some agencies concentrate on placing children from the United States, whereas others place children from orphanages overseas. Some agencies do both. Some are sectarian (religious, such as Catholic, Lutheran, Jewish, Methodist, Latter Day Saints, etc.); others are not. In most states, the adoption agency must be a nonprofit organization.

Independent Adoption

Most states allow "independent adoption," which means the adoption is arranged not by an adoption agency but by an attorney or by the adoptive parents and birthparents themselves. In such cases, an attorney can assist with the legal work. In some states, attorneys can match prospective adoptive parents to birthparents.

Most states also require that in an independent adoption, a social worker or an adoption agency will perform a "home study" of a prospective adoptive couple. This refers to an investigation of the couple and a recommendation for or against allowing them to adopt. Few people are turned down to adopt.

Some people arrange their own independent adoptions of children from other countries. A home study is still required by the Immigration and Naturalization Service, but the family can handle many details.

THE HOME STUDY PROCESS

If you do decide to adopt, you will generally need to undergo a detailed special background investigation, usually called a home study. This process unnerves many people, but it is quite survivable.

You Can't Hide from Their Prying Eyes
(or So You Think)

In most states (and in all intercountry adoptions) a home study is required to adopt a child. A home study is a complete investigation by a social worker of your background and your health history. In addition, you will be asked many questions about yourself, why you want to adopt a child, what you expect from parenting, and much more.

Most social workers receive on-the-job training, so what they ask you is based on what the agency wants them to ask you, within reason. Most will try to get to know you as a person and learn about your motivations in adopting a child. Their questions are designed to elicit the information they need to write a report on you and a recommendation about whether you should be approved to adopt.

Social Worker Stereotypes May Scare You

Maxine Chalker, M.S.W., director of Adoptions From the Heart, an adoption agency in Ardmore, Pennsylvania, thinks some people choose attorneys over agencies because they are afraid of agencies. "I think they still have that old stereotype of a social worker in laced-up shoes with her hair in a bun, who comes to their house with white gloves and a clipboard."

In addition, Chalker says, many people say they don't want counseling. "What do they think we do, look into their brain cells? They think we're going to force them to tell their innermost secrets, but they don't have to say anything they don't want to say." She says that people also dislike home studies because of the cost involved. You need to understand that the cost of the home study is for a complete evaluation of your family, not just a few meetings.

Do most people "pass"? Almost everyone is approved in the home study process. Only a few are turned down, the usual reasons being a history of alcohol or drug abuse, serious emotional or psychological problems, or other issues that could impair parenting abilities. Sometimes the social worker will recommend further counseling before you adopt.

If you are an exceptionally private person who does not want people to ask personal questions, the home study could be difficult for you. Even very confident extroverted people can be daunted by the process. Not that the process is so awful, but rather that many people are so worried about saying or doing the "wrong thing" that they make it hard on themselves.

If you are a very quiet and private person and don't think you would want to handle such invasions, then you could have problems with a home study. On the other hand, your desire to adopt may be so intense that you can overcome such obstacles. A key factor is How bad do you want to adopt? I have seen very shy people succeed at adoption—they were highly motivated. Part Two of this book will help you do some self-analysis—and some of it will be fun!

PART TWO

LOOKING INWARD— QUESTIONS TO ASK YOURSELF

3

TAKING A LOOK
AT YOURSELF
AS A POSSIBLE PARENT

The decision to adopt involves not only the choice to enhance your family with an adopted child but also the choice to be a parent. This chapter discusses the transition from no children to becoming a parent, whether your child is born to you or adopted by you. Also discussed are key aspects of effective parenting traits and skills, such as effective listening, exhibiting empathy, flexibility/adaptability, and patience and conflict resolution skills. You may already be good at them, but if these traits are not your strong suit, you need to be willing to work on them.

In addition, adoptive parenting as a subject in and of itself is covered, because some challenges are unique to adoptive parenting.

"PRACTICING" PARENTHOOD

Before I get into the areas of how children can change your life, I'd like to say that a surprising number of people who adopt children have virtually no experience with infants or small children. If you've never babysat a child—or did so only when you were sixteen and you're now thirty-six—it's a good idea to get some practice under your belt.

Although you'll never feel about someone else's children as you will feel about your child, volunteer to babysit the children of your relatives and friends. Don't take on a really huge bite—if you're completely inexperienced, do *not* volunteer to watch your brother's four kids so he and his wife can go on vacation to New Zealand for three weeks. Very bad idea.

Instead, volunteer to watch the children for a few hours, and slowly build up your tolerance level for them. Perhaps you could volunteer at a church nursery school or some other group. Find out what it's like to have a small child who wants what she or he wants NOW and cannot be reasoned with. See how you deal with this and discover what areas you may need to work on.

HOW CHILDREN CHANGE YOUR LIFE

Children change your personal life, they affect your marital relationship (even your sex life; don't forget to lock the bedroom door after your child starts walking—and as long as your child lives at home with you—if you want privacy!), your social relationships, family interactions, and even your job. Their influence in your entire life is extremely pervasive.

An infant will probably have the greatest influence on you. Most new mothers and some fathers (biological and adoptive) report that the responsibility of round-the-clock parenthood is quite a shock. You're always "on." Unlike a job that you leave in the evening, parenting an infant is continuous. (Parenting responsibilities are continuous with older children, too, but children over age five or six will be attending school all day and sleeping through the night, so the parenting experience is very different.)

Even if you place your baby in day care, the child will usually be with *you* all night long, and either you or your partner will need to attend to the crying child and fulfill his or her needs—once you figure out what they are. Sometimes newly adoptive parents panic because they just cannot figure out why the baby is crying—she doesn't want a bottle, her diaper is dry, she doesn't seem sick, so what is it? They may worry that biological parents would just *know* what to do.

This panicky feeling is also very common among new biological parents. They have no magical knowledge, despite what you may have read. Everyone has to learn by trial and error and experience.

Your Job

Many working women find that they think about their children while at work and they worry about job-related problems when at home. It's hard to compartmentalize the two. And yet, as much as possible, it's important to think about work when you're on the job and think about your child when you are with him or her. This is very easy to say and can be very hard to do, especially if you're a little worried about those sniffles your child had this morning.

Many women find that they need to cut back on their working hours. They may have to leave early or during the day to take their child to the physician, dentist, or other appointments. They can't count on taking work home to do at night, because often their child will demand attention then. After all, they were gone all day . . .

Another common work problem is finding good child care. First, do you choose a day care center or hire a person to come into your home? You must evaluate the available caregivers and weigh the various pros and cons of different alternatives. For example, you may prefer to have someone care for your child in your own home, but a major disadvantage is that if the person becomes ill or unavailable for some reason, and your backup babysitters can't help you out, you may have to stay home. Despite the major meeting set for today, and despite the key issues you planned to cover at work, when it comes to caring for your child, the responsibility ultimately will lie with you, the parent.

Another factor is that you may get little sympathy from others who see themselves on the fast track and perceive you (if you're a woman) on the "mommy track." In fact, if you are a single person, you might receive some outright resentment, for a variety of reasons: disapproval of singles adopting, disapproval of single parents in general, and so forth. It's noteworthy that divorced single men who parent children are seen much more positively than are women— although single men who adopt nonrelatives may be viewed suspiciously by some.

Your Marital Relationship

One thing both biological and adoptive parents learn (or should learn) as their child grows up, is that parents need private time together. One advantage of adoptive parenting is that although the new mom may be tired, she does not also have to cope with the hormonal changes of new motherhood and she can also have sex right away if she wants to—no waiting period for the body to heal. Of course, keep in mind that many late nights spent feeding the baby can wear you out, too.

When the child, whatever age, first comes into your lives, your marital relationship will be affected because both of you now have a third person to consider. Sometimes you'll have to subordinate your needs to the needs of the child; for example, you want to go on vacation, you've planned it and maybe even paid for it, but the child becomes too ill to go, so you have to cancel.

If you both work, you must decide on a plan for who stays home with the child when she or he is ill and can't go to a babysitter or day care center. Some people take turns; some go by whose job is currently most demanding—the one with the less demanding job takes on the child care. But unless you both agree on how to handle this situation, it can lead to hurt feelings and arguments: "You don't think my job is important!" and so on.

You may also find differences in how you each feel the child should be parented, and you may often unconsciously fall back into the same patterns used by your parents. This may be very different from how your spouse was parented.

The pocketbook can also affect your marital relationship. Less money often means fewer opportunities. You may not be able to buy that new car this year or remodel your family room or spend the money on a vacation.

Arguments over money are very common between couples and you may find them more frequent when the children come. A person who was formerly frugal may decide that no expense should be spared for the child. For example, you may think that your daughter really *needs* costly handmade dresses, whereas your spouse believes that clothes bought in the local discount store are just fine. Your spouse may think that what your family needs most is a new boat, and you disagree.

So you and your spouse may well need to rethink your priorities over money and expenditures. Children are expensive! On the other hand, if you truly yearn for children, they are infinitely valuable and no amount of dollars in the bank would be an adequate substitute for the joy of parenting.

Your Free Time

As a parent, you'll find that your free time is much less free. Rather than dashing off to dinner and a movie, you may find yourself doing laundry, cleaning up baby (or big kid) spills, and attending to a broad array of child care duties and responsibilities. (And the fun parts, too.)

Lifestyle Choices Are Child-Driven

Many areas of your life will be directly impacted if you become a parent. For example, the kind of car you drive, where you live, and where (or if) you go on vacation are often directly affected by whether you become a parent. Many people choose to relocate at some point after parenthood, so their children can live in a safer neighborhood or go to a better school. You may find yourself going to Disneyland rather than to Las Vegas on your vacation—which might be fine for you unless you find amusement parks jarring. If you adopt an infant, you'll need a car that can fit in a baby seat and still have room for all the paraphernalia needed to take an infant out, even for a short period.

Plenty of Pluses to Parenthood

On the plus side, when you become a parent, you join the "club" of other parents at work, and many begin to see you as they see themselves—having all the trials, tribulations, and joys of raising a child. If parenthood is valued at your company, then you may rise a notch or so in the general viewpoint of fellow employees.

Few joys surpass parenthood in its special moments—the ones you think about readily, such as birthdays, and the little unexpected ones, such as being presented with handmade items by your child or hearing your son or daughter say, "I love you." My older kids are in their late teens, but I still have gifts that they made in kindergarten.

You may also find yourself appreciating "the moment" far more. Rather than feeling chained to the career rat race, you allow yourself to take precious minutes to appreciate things you've taken for granted but are now seeing through your child's eyes: the moon, a bright sunny day, a butterfly.

Parenthood has too many pluses to cite them all, but many adoptive parents say that adopting their child was one of the best decisions they ever made.

IS YOUR LIFESTYLE CHILD-READY?

Are you the type of person who loves to travel a lot? Do you like to act impulsively, deciding at a moment's notice to go to a hot new restaurant—one that's three hours from your home? Or are you more of a stay-at-home person, content to putter about in your garden or try a new recipe?

No matter what kind of person you are, your life will inevitably change if you become a parent. The woman who loves to pack up and go whenever she feels like it will need to factor in the child's needs, as well as the countless items required if the child is an infant (diapers, bottles, food, wipers, toys, strollers, etc.). The man who'd rather stay home will find his world enlarged, even if somewhat unwillingly, by the needs of a growing child who participates in sports, piano lessons, Cub Scouts or Brownies, and on and on.

Your life doesn't have to be and shouldn't be completely ruled by your child. But the child's needs should be considered as much as possible.

TRAITS OF A GOOD PARENT

From my experience both as a parent and as a researcher of parenting topics, I have come to believe that good parents need to possess or to develop certain basic skills in order to succeed at the tough job of parenting: ability to listen, empathy, flexibility/adaptability, patience, conflict resolution, self-confidence and self-acceptance. These are also skills that many social workers look at when evaluating prospective parents, although all social workers probably don't identify each skill exactly as I have listed them. Where do you stand on these traits?

Ability to Listen

One skill ignored by many is the one I list first: the ability to listen. Most people assume that anyone who can hear will readily receive and discern what is said to them. The problem, however, is that too many of us don't listen effectively because as the other person speaks, we're too busy framing what we want to say *back* to the other person. Or we drift off and start thinking about something else altogether. By the time we come "back," it's often impossible to pick up the thread of what's being said.

Good listening is important to parenting because many times children will give you a distorted or confused picture of what is going on and sometimes, especially when very young, they will lie or exaggerate. You need to have or develop the ability to listen to what your child is saying and also grasp the emotion and underlying message behind what is being said. An obvious example is the small boy standing with both hands behind his back, looking very guilty. "I don't have NOTHING!" he insists. But you know who took the cookies. This is an easy one, but it gets harder and harder.

If you're not an effective listener now, it is certainly possible to become one, and you have plenty of chances to practice. Here are a few basic hints.

- Try to determine what is the main idea. If you are given many details, what is the common denominator, or what is the speaker trying to convey to you?
- Try to identify words or phrases that annoy you and trip you up in listening. For example, one of mine is "You're dead meat" to indicate that the person you're speaking to is in trouble. Once you know your own red flags, you can gain better control and avoid getting stuck in thinking about how irritated you are, thus missing information.
- Try to avoid focusing on the person's appearance. This is *hard* for a parent. If you are too focused on Tiffany's messy hair, you can't listen to her tell you why her teacher is pleased with her, and you will both end up frustrated. She's trying to tell you something good, but you're not only *not* listening, you're responding negatively. Everyone, child or adult, wants to be heard.
- If you can't listen now because you're upset about something, ask the person if you can discuss this later. And *do* discuss it later.
- Ask questions to clarify points and rephrase back to the person what you think he or she has said. "So it sounds like you are saying that Mrs. Jones is upset that you damaged her tulips, but that you really didn't mean to do it. Is that right?"
- Try to determine the speaker's emotions—are they confused, happy, sad, or what? Tiffany in the earlier example not only wanted her mother to hear her, but she also wanted her mother to hear the emotion she was expressing of pride and happiness in being recognized for an achievement. Asking questions is one good way to find out, as in the other example of the tulips. Many people make the mistake of listening briefly to a child's problems and then launching into a lecture about something that happened to them—in the Ice Age, as far as the child is concerned. It's important to try to understand and accept the

emotions that the child is feeling, even if you don't feel them yourself and never did.

- Try to empathize with the speaker. But resist the tendency to launch into a long-winded trip down memory lane (the old "I trudged to school six miles in the blizzard" kind of thing).

Empathy

Can you identify with the feelings and problems of others, even if they are very unlike emotions or problems you've ever had? Children in our constantly changing world may experience a wide array of problems that you never faced as a child, so don't assume it's a heavenly experience to be a child today.

Think back to your own school years. Can you remember how it felt when someone embarrassed you in school? Do you recall how you felt when your parents were very pleased or very angry with you? What about when you told the truth but your parents didn't believe you? The important point here is to think back and empathize with *yourself* as a child. Is that possible? Or are you too ready to call yourself names or tell yourself that bad things never happened to you, that your life was just a perfect idyllic dream? (No one's childhood is perfect, no matter how nice the parents were.)

This is a good exercise to help you move into true consideration of parenting. If you can forgive your own silly (and serious) errors that you made as a child and as an adult, then you probably can also empathize with your child's mistakes as well.

Flexibility/Adaptability

Are you somewhat rigid, a person who plans to leave at 2 P.M. and by golly, you leave at 2 P.M. no matter what happens? Watch out with parenting! Children have accidents, they procrastinate, and they forget a lot—which are only a few of the reasons why it's important to have a flexible and adaptable outlook. This doesn't mean you have to react to everything your children want, giving it to them exactly when they want it. But you need to have or develop the capacity to rethink your position based on new information and make new strategies or tactics to solve problems that aren't readily solved with old ways.

You will also need to be adaptable as your child grows up; for example, coping strategies that work with the toddler or preschooler are usually ineffectual with the eight-year-old and useless with the adolescent. Thus, you will periodically need to adjust your thinking and continue to work on your parenting skills—the parent-child relationship is a dynamic and changing one.

Patience

I think most people would agree that patience is definitely a virtue in parenting. Do you tend to fly off the handle, or can you hold your breath or count to ten or use other tactics to control your emotions? This is important, because children can be the most wonderful creatures and the most aggravating ones as well—and sometimes they can be *both*, within a dizzyingly short period of time. They will test you just to see how you react.

How have you dealt with frustration, annoying people, and difficult problems in the past? Do you throw papers up in the air and stalk out? Do you spew out whatever angry words are in your mind? You will need to develop patience, should you choose to become a parent.

Even good parents sometimes lose their temper with children. Parents can and should apologize when they are wrong. In addition, you can't expect yourself to always be calm in front of your child. No one can keep up a front like that. It's okay for your child to see you upset once in a while. However, if you are arguing with your spouse or another person in another family, it's best if you do so in private.

Conflict Resolution

Good conflict resolution skills are important, too. If you want a serene lifestyle, don't become a parent. Even the most well behaved children get into scrapes, become upset over what you might consider nothing, and generate plenty of conflict. Your conflict resolution skills—or the ones you develop—will become important to you. Think about how you handle conflicts now. Do you expect others to solve all your problems, or do you primarily wish them away? Or do you try to solve the ones that can be worked on?

It's key to learn how to identify the problem *behind* the behavior and take corrective actions to resolve it whenever possible. Conflict resolution will also be important if you will be a two-parent family because sometimes your spouse will not agree with you on how to parent the child. It's a good idea to present a "united front" to the child and do your arguing behind the scenes, if you can.

Do loud arguments throw you into a tailspin? Do you find yourself developing a migraine or a stomachache when the even keel of your life gets very wavy? In this case, it's a good idea to ask yourself if you are willing and able to develop the skills needed to become a good parent—and to accept that sometimes, no matter what you do, the child (or you) will be upset for a while and that is just the way it is.

Self-Confidence and Self-Acceptance

A healthy self-image is important for a parent. Of course, virtually every parent questions his or her parenting skills sometimes, but if you must agonize over every trivial decision—"Should I put her in the snowsuit or the lighter jacket? Oh no, I can't decide!"—then parenting any child will be tough on the child and tough on you.

If you are more likely to consider your successes and not continually dwell on your failures or mistakes, you may have the self-acceptance level needed for good parenting. In fact, studies have revealed that parents with good self-images are ultimately more accepting of their adopted children. (I suspect this is probably true for people who parent biological children as well.) Conversely, if you tend to be hypercritical of yourself, you are more likely to be unaccepting of a child's mistakes. Children do need discipline. But they also need to know that your love is unconditional and that even if they are "bad," you will correct them but you will still love them.

In one study of eighty couples who adopted 121 children, the parents were tested on self-acceptance and on parental acceptance of their children. Researchers found that the higher the parents scored on self-acceptance, the higher also were their scores on parental acceptance of their children.

It can be difficult to evaluate this trait in yourself, but you can ask yourself a few basic questions—for example, when you make a mistake, do you find yourself obsessing on the ninety-eight ways that you could have and *should* have done (whatever) differently? Does it matter whether it was a major mistake with lasting impact or a trivial matter? If you think that you may be somewhat perfectionistic, you may wish to seek some counseling to work on this trait and improve your self-acceptance level—and to resolve whatever issues may be impinging on or impairing your self-acceptance. Once resolved, you may find yourself ready to plunge into parenthood!

HOW BECOMING AN ADOPTIVE PARENT IS DIFFERENT

All children need food, clothing, shelter, and plenty of love. It doesn't matter whether they were adopted or not. But because our society does emphasize differences, and because adoption is often depicted negatively by the news media and on television, sometimes children who were adopted wonder about whether they are as good as everyone else—that is, everyone who was not adopted.

Of course, adoptive parents tell their children that they love them. In fact, sometimes adoptive parents are overachievers in this area, telling the children too often that they are special, important, and so forth.

Another reason that adoption makes parenting different is that children do wonder why they were adopted and sometimes they ask questions about birthparents, even when the situation was an open adoption.

Some differences between adoptive and biological parenting are the result of the nature of adoption and of problems that the child may have faced in a foster home or an orphanage before being adopted. Other problems occur as a result of the societal stigma against adoption, based rather heavily on how the media depicts adopted children. (Dr. George Gerbner of the Annenberg School of Communications at the University of Pennsylvania did a study on adoption and the media in 1988, illustrating a distinct bias against adoption among an array of national media.)

Perceived Differences

Many adoptive moms have complained that biological mothers have told them that it is impossible to know how a "real" mother feels unless you give birth to a child. How biological mothers can know this, if they have not adopted a child, is a point worth making; however, many people think biology is all.

Consequently, adoptive parents can sometimes start to feel inadequate and actually begin to have doubts and fears about their own parenting abilities. What they do not know is that nearly *all* new parents are afraid that they will be inadequate or make mistakes that will somehow traumatize their children. This is especially true when biological moms bring home their newborns from the hospital. If the mom has never cared for an infant before, she must learn through trial and error, daily experience, the help of her mother and other mothers, and from information in books.

After the Baby Comes Home

Sometimes biological mothers suffer from postpartum depression, making it difficult or impossible for them to fully care for the new baby. Presuming that a full recovery is eventually made, they can later give the child the attention he or she needs. What is not widely known is that some adoptive moms feel a kind of letdown after adoption, which may be in large part caused by the enormous fatigue associated with being a new parent.

In one unique study reported in the June 1991 issue of *American Family Physician*, researchers compared the well-being of biological mothers to that of adoptive mothers (and to that of a control group with no children). All the women were married. They found that the adoptive mothers and biological mothers were both tired and not eager to return to work. Both also spent less time on household chores and social and recreational activities, compared to the women with no children. Interestingly, the adoptive mothers had the fewest physical complaints and the best mental health of all *three* groups.

Parental Expectations

How the child is expected to act, as an adopted child and sometimes as a member of a different racial or ethnic group, is of course a concern unique to adoptive parents. For example, some people believe that if you adopt a Chinese infant, that child will automatically grow up to be obedient, submissive, dedicated to studies, and so forth—just like the stereotype of Chinese children who are parented by Chinese parents. Forget these stereotypes and any expectations you may have that are based on race or ethnicity. An adopted child, especially one adopted as an infant, will reflect the impact and culture of the adoptive parents.

Even when deciding what to name the child, your covert expectations can surface. For example, naming your adopted child James William Stone IV could place some considerably heavy baggage on that child. It could also cause some resentment among family members because the child is not a genetic child. They may feel he is not entitled to the name, whether they tell you this or not.

Societal Stigmas Against Adoption

The general negative bias in our society against adoption can affect how adopted children are treated. For example, if teachers believe in the "poor little adopted child" myth, they may bend over backward to make life easy—too easy—for the child.

In addition, if you are white and adopt an African American child or another child of color, you and your child will encounter racism that is not so benevolent as that associated with the Chinese stereotypes. For example, some people may overtly or covertly act upon their beliefs that certain racial or ethnic groups are not as smart or industrious as are others.

Even the mere fact of racial differences brings up issues. Jean Nelson-Erichsen and her husband adopted their twin daughters from Colombia twenty-four years ago, and she says the questions don't stop. People still ask her daughters, "What are you?"—meaning what race. When the daughters respond that they are Colombian, some people press them about what percentage Indian they are. (They don't know and most other Colombians don't know either, according to Nelson-Erichsen.) This TV-talk-show mentality—that everyone wants to disclose everything personal about themselves—can be aggravating. Study after study on transracial adoptions indicate that most adoptive parents and their children—despite encountering some difficulties—are very glad that the adoption happened.

Your Own Underlying Beliefs About Adoption

I think parents' beliefs about adoption in general are important, too. For example, I have talked to some adoptive parents who are convinced that adoption is a terrible loss for the child, even if she or he was adopted as a two-day-old infant. They believe that the child will inevitably grow up to feel rejected because the biological mother "didn't want her child," and that nothing they can say or do will assuage this.

I wonder if such mothers have ever heard of the self-fulfilling prophecy, If you believe in something strongly enough, you can make it happen. It's highly likely that parents who "know" that adoption is inevitably a terrible loss for an adopted person will convey this belief to their child and, unwittingly, make him or her feel inferior because of the adoption.

If the child is older when adopted, the situation is different. There may well be issues of loss; for example, if the child had been in foster care for several years, then he or she probably developed an attachment to the foster parents, and will need time to perceive you as the parent. Some adoptive parents allow visits between the foster parents and the child—visits that taper off and ultimately end, but that permit the child to still see the foster parents as he or she develops a relationship with the new parents.

Some psychologists, social workers, and psychiatrists speak and write about the inevitable and terrible "losses" of adoption for every adopted person. My position is that there is no way to prove or disprove that all adopted people feel a piercing loss. When someone tells you that *all* people in any group feel one way or another, particularly when the group is very large (at least 6 million adopted children and adults reside in the United States), warning flags should go up and alarms should sound in your head.

SELF-EVALUATION QUESTIONNAIRE FOR PEOPLE CONSIDERING ADOPTION

One exercise that might help you before you answer the following questions is to imagine that you have adopted a child twenty years ago. What profession is your child in? What does your adult child look like? It might also help if you jot down these ideas, providing as complete a description as possible of your future child, all grown up. Then move on to the questions. Be honest! No one but you needs to see your answers. Write them in pencil if you wish.

Answer each question with *low, average,* or *high. Average* refers to what you see as a moderate response. There are no right answers or wrong answers to this self-rating questionnaire; it is just a tool to help you evaluate yourself and identify where possible strengths and weaknesses that relate to parenthood may lie.

1. How important is physical attractiveness to you? For example, do you exercise regularly? If you believe that you judge yourself and others almost solely on nonphysical traits, you'd rate yourself as *low*; whereas, for example, if you are a woman, and you think it's important to wear makeup even if you're just making a quick trip to the supermarket, then you're a *high*. If you are a man, and you believe it's important to shave on Saturday morning before going to the convenience store for milk, you're a *high* too.

2. How important is academic achievement? What if your child has problems in school? Suppose that your child's grades are not so good—do you think that you could deal with that? Will you assume that your child just isn't "trying hard enough"? If you believe that school performance is critically important to success in life, then you're a *high*. If this is not of paramount concern to you, you're a *low*.

3. What about your adult child, as you have envisioned him or her? (Remember, I told you to do this, earlier in this section.) Do you see your child as a doctor or lawyer or other professional? Now switch gears, and imagine that he's a hair stylist and she's a janitor—how would you feel about that? If you think that a professional or high-paying career is important, then you're a *high*. If career status is not a big issue for you, then rate yourself as a *low*.

4. Are you a fighter, an assertive person when you need to be? Have you ever fought "the system" when you were wronged? Have you spoken up on behalf of others or do you find yourself more likely to look the other way?

5. When you make plans and something happens to make them go awry, do you become upset or do you adjust to the new situation? Low adaptability means that you just can't cope with change; high adaptability means that you can make changes without skipping a beat.

6. Are you a neat person compared to others? Do all the hangers go the same way in your closet? Are you always on time? Rate

your own ability to be orderly: *low* means that you don't really think a lot about how much "neatness counts"; *high* means that you are generally much tidier than others.

7. When things go wrong, does it really get you down? Do you find yourself crying at every movie? Do you stay upset for long periods after a disagreement with your spouse or a friend? Do you find yourself unable to eat or sleep if you are upset? Or are you the kind of person who is rather placid, nothing bothers you, and you always sleep through the night? *Low* in this measure of emotional stability means that you are easily upset; *high* means that you believe you have a high level of emotional control.

8. If you are married, what's your relationship with your spouse like? If you are not married, how about relationships with family members or friends? Do you believe that no matter what, your family will love and support you? Rate how important your relationships with others are to you, with *low* being that you have few relationships and are quite self-sufficient and *high* being that you have extremely close ties to the people who matter to you.

9. How important is good physical health to you? Is it very important that any child you adopt have minimal health problems? Could you accept it if the healthy child develops problems? Rate the importance of good health to you, with *low* meaning that you feel most health issues can be taken in stride, and *high* meaning that you could not cope with a child with a serious problem.

10. How about emotional problems? Do you think you would have difficulty dealing with a child who developed a psychological problem? *Low* means that you feel you could handle most emotional problems, and *high* means that you would find such problems too stressful.

11. In considering your financial status honestly (nobody thinks he or she has enough money), would you regard yourself as financially secure? Or are you more or less living on the edge, moneywise? Are you maxed out on all your credit cards? Rate your financial stability, with *low* being that you are living day to day and *high* being that you have clear financial plans that you've already begun carrying out (IRAs, retirement plans, etc.).

12. Consider the amount of time, both on and off the job, that you spend on work and work-related activities. Do you believe that

work concerns consume a great deal of your time, a moderate amount, or very little? A child will create demands on your time as well. Rate yourself in terms of how much time you feel you could take off from work tasks. Is your free time a *high* or a *low*?

13. Is religion an important issue in your life? How do you think you would rate the importance of religion if you adopted a child? Rate the importance of religion in your life from *low* (not important at all) to *high* (very important and integral to your life).

14. Is it very important for you to adopt a child of a particular sex— you want only a girl or only a boy? Rate yourself *low* if it doesn't matter at all whether the child you adopt is male or female. Rate yourself *high* if you feel you could only adopt a child who is the gender you prefer.

How to Rate Yourself

Let's consider each item.

1. *Physical attractiveness.* Whether they admit it, some people think that physical attractiveness is very important. It's not bad to try to look nice, but it can become a problem if you tend to judge others primarily on the basis of appearance. Many people do this. One parent who had adopted transracially was horrified when another person told her that she should have her African American daughter's nose "fixed" when she was older so she would be attractive. Obviously, this was a racist remark, but it also reflected one person's view of beauty.

   You are not "bad" if you see having a physical disability as being problematic; however, be honest with yourself and know that if you find nonstandard appearance a problem, then you should not adopt a child who has one.

   If you rated physical attractiveness as high, you should think over whether you should adopt any child. If you believe that looking very good (or maybe perfect) is of paramount importance, then you may have the tendency to project the importance of physical attractiveness onto the child, particularly if the child is of the same gender as you are. The gorgeous infant or toddler could become a plain-looking teenager, but she or he still needs your love and acceptance.

If you said that attractiveness doesn't matter at all, then you should rethink this and make sure you're being honest with yourself. (As with all questions, "average" reflects the middle ground.)

In addition, some people decide against adoption because they want a child who looks like their spouse. (Interestingly, there is no guarantee that a biological child will resemble your partner.) If it is very important to you that your child resemble you or your spouse, then consider adoption very carefully. It's one thing if you want to adopt a child of the same race or gender as you. It's another if you want to specify hair color, eye color, and so forth. Such "specifications" can be indicative of perfectionistic and unreasonable expectations.

2. *Achievement.* Setting and accomplishing major goals is important to some individuals who rate their success in school, at work, and at other ventures. Of course, it's good for children to have goals and to learn the joy of succeeding at them. But what if a child is basically an average student—no matter how hard he or she tries? If you rated achievement as a *high*, will you be disappointed if Mary brings home a few Cs (or worse) on her report card but seems to be doing her best?

On the other hand, we do live in an achievement-oriented society and children do learn by overcoming obstacles. If you rated achievement's importance as *low* can you provide a stimulating environment and can you find joy in your child's successes and commiserate with his or her other less-than-successful results? Think about it.

Also consider the attitude toward academic achievement within your own extended family—your parents and your siblings. This, too, could play an important part in your attitudes and in the attitudes of your spouse.

3. *Career status.* How important is it to you that your child follow your career path or that of your spouse's? Do you think that if you're an attorney, the child should also be a professional when he grows up? But what if your child grows up to be a good plumber or successful truck driver—but not the brain surgeon you dreamed about? Would you be disappointed then? Not every child can become a successful professional. Our society also needs "worker bees."

4. *Assertiveness.* Parents must also inevitably act as advocates for their children at some points. Thus, assertiveness is an important quality in a parent and one you will need to develop if you don't already have it. Maybe it's a teacher who seems to be unfair to a child or maybe it's another child or even a physician—in any case, you'll have to deal with the problem.

   Presuming that the problem seems valid and that the treatment truly is unfair, could you argue on your child's behalf or are you somewhat of a shrinking violet? Answering *high* could indicate that you are a rather combative person; *low* could indicate a shy person. Keep in mind, however, that in many cases, even a rather retiring person can become a virtual tiger if his or her child is threatened.

5. *Adaptability.* Your ability to be flexible is a very important aspect of parenthood. Your life will change a lot if you adopt a child, and many new and different situations will present themselves to you. Can you switch gears and react to what has happened, or do you tend to become stuck on the unfairness of it all?

   If you rated yourself as *low* in Question 5, you may need to think about how to help yourself become more flexible and more open to new situations. For example, maybe you planned to go out to dinner with your spouse. The reservations are made, and you're looking forward to it. Then your child vomits violently. You feel his head and discover that he's feverish. You cancel your evening out. Would you feel as if life is just so unfair, and would you dwell on this for hours?

   Flexibility is also important in day-to-day parenting of children. For example, inevitably, children have many emotions and also inspire a broad range in others, including parents. When you see a child having a temper tantrum in the supermarket, do you automatically assume the mother is a stupid jerk because of the child's behavior? Think harder—you may well face the same situation.

   If you can understand that children often misbehave when they are sick or tired (or both), then you can better deal with such problems. If you rated yourself as *low* in this question, you need to work on your flexibility skills.

6. *Organizational abilities.* How much does neatness count in your life? An ability to organize is certainly an asset, but on the other

hand, if you are intent on categorizing and labeling everything, you may find parenthood difficult.

Children are chaotic beings and they create lots of messes, both physical (toys everywhere) and emotional (the previously mentioned temper tantrum is only one example). They may have great difficulty creating "hospital corners" when they make their beds, and they may lose things. Some children have attention deficit disorder and are particularly prone to creating chaos. If you rated yourself *high* here, and you're a person who must have all the *t*s crossed and the *i*s dotted in your life, you may need to think harder about parenthood before undertaking this endeavor.

On the other hand, children do need structure and dependability, and if you are too flexible about mealtimes, bedtimes, and other issues, children can become anxious and upset. One psychiatrist evaluated a set of twins (not adopted) who lived in an extremely chaotic environment. She noted that when the twins were in the playroom, they dedicated their entire time to organizing toys into categories, rather than playing with the toys.

7. *Emotional stability.* How readily do you handle the ups and downs of daily life? No one is happy all the time. But if you are springloaded to react to the daily vicissitudes of life (a *low* on the emotional control question), then you will find parenting to be especially challenging unless you learn to deal with this.

Conversely, you do need to have the ability to react to your children, rather than to have a "flat affect" or no reaction to anything. If you are a *high* on the emotional control scale, do you also have your moments of spontaneity and silliness? Children learn from your behavior, and if you are very rigidly controlled, this is problematic as well.

8. *Relationships.* Your relationships with other people are important indicators to your future success. If you are estranged from most or all family members and are constantly arguing with your spouse (a *low* on our questionnaire), it does not bode well for success at parenting. Some experts believe that close relationships with children are directly affected by the condition of your marital relationship—the better the marriage, the happier the child.

On the other hand, are you *very* close (a *high*) to some people? Do you and your mother call each other every day, and if not, do you feel distraught? Do you worry yourself sick if your sister must go on a short business trip? Having very close relations with family members can mean that the adopted child gets shut out. Also, if your family disapproves of the child or hates the idea of adoption, could you disengage for a while (or longer) for your child's sake?

9. *Good health.* Of course, we all want to enjoy good health, and we want our children to be well, too. But if a child becomes seriously ill, could you deal with this? Some people find sickness to be impossibly stressful and nearly go to pieces when a child is sick or develops a chronic illness. If you rated yourself *high* on the importance of good physical health, can you handle ill health?

10. *Emotional stability.* Although some parents can manage physical ailments—even serious ones—quite well, trying to deal with emotional problems may derail them. Do you think you could handle it if your child were diagnosed with attention deficit disorder or another emotional problem? Maybe you aren't sure—but it's worth thinking about.

11. *Your financial status.* It's a good idea to take into account your financial "health." You need not be on the high end of financial success; however, any adoption agency or adoption professional will look at your financial status to try to determine if you will be able to afford the many costs of parenting a child, which can be a real drain sometimes.

12. *Available time.* Do you really have the time to raise a child? And if not, could you (and would you) adjust your (*high* work priority) schedule so that you will be able to dedicate the necessary time to parenting tasks?

    Remember, you should not be expected to give up your entire life and quit your job if you adopt a child. On the other hand, it's inevitable that you'll need to make adjustments, and readjusting your work schedule may be necessary.

13. *Religion's role in your life.* If you and your spouse have not been engaged in religious activities, do you think this would change if you adopted a child? And if so, whose religion would predominate, if you and your spouse were raised in different religions?

14. *Importance of adopting a girl or boy.* This was a trick question because it doesn't evaluate any particular trait. But I think it's an

issue that needs to be considered by prospective adoptive parents. Some people request a specific gender—for example, perhaps they wish to adopt a girl because they already have three boys and want to be sure their next child is a girl.

If it's very important to you that you adopt a child of a particular sex, you may find that a U.S. adoption of an infant is difficult. After all, even sonograms can be wrong. I know an adoptive mom who had the nursery painted all pink and put ruffles everywhere because the birthmother's doctor said she was going to have a girl. Somehow, the doctor was wrong and the baby was a boy. But it was okay—the couple repainted the room blue and threw out the flounces, and no parents could be more devoted to their son.

If choosing gender is important to you, you may need to seek to adopt an older child or baby.

What if you think that you did "bad" on this test—you're too organized, not very flexible, love to look nice, and think that high SAT scores are one of the most important things in the world? Do not abandon hope! Once you identify possible problem areas, you can better explore them. People can (and do) change when they become parents. If you are willing to work at whatever possible problem areas you may have, in many cases, you can succeed. Remember: You don't have to be perfect to adopt a child. Just don't expect the child to be perfect either.

4

BONDING, ATTACHMENT, AND ENTITLEMENT

Your ability to create a close relationship between you and your adopted child, which some people call bonding, as well as your feeling of entitlement—that you are the child's "real" parent and deserve to be seen as such—are very important topics. Some people believe that if you can't make contact with a child in the first few hours after birth, then you can't bond with that child. Others believe that only biological parents can truly bond with a child. Many social workers, mental health professionals and I disagree with these views. I am an adoptive mother who has bonded with her child, and I have also been privileged to personally observe bonding that took place between other adoptive parents and their children.

DEFINING BONDING
AND ATTACHMENT

What do these terms mean, and why should you care about them anyway if you haven't yet made up your mind about adoption?

The terms bonding and attachment have a wide variety of interpretations and definitions. I believe that bonding refers to the presumed interactive process that leads to a psychological attachment between a parent and child—usually referring to a mother and child. This attachment is a mutual relationship that seems special. Thus I see bonding as the *process* of forming a close relationship between two individuals and attachment as the *result*.

Merriam-Webster's Medical Desk Dictionary defines bonding this way: "The formation of a close personal relationship . . . between a mother and child . . . esp. through frequent or constant association . . ." (Attachment was defined only in a physical sense, not in an emotional or psychological one.)

In a 1996 article on attachment and separation in young children, Tiffany Field defines attachment as "a relationship between two beings which integrates their physiological and behavioral systems." Field believes that people have multiple attachments through life, although she says, "Attachment theory generally has been limited to the primary attachment figure and child during brief stressful situations."

Pediatrician Jerri Ann Jenista, M.D., editor of *Adoption/Medical News* and adoptive mother of five children, thinks the terms bonding and attachment are far too loosely defined. She says that most people are referring to the developing of reciprocal relationships. Such relationships can occur between parents and children as well as between spouses, friends, and others.

Attaching to an Older Child

Attachment can (and usually does) occur between adoptive parents and their child. It is usually assumed that the bonding process will take time, and the older the child, the longer the process will take. In most cases, the older adopted child has been abused or neglected and has already had many negative experiences. So why should the child trust you right away? Older children need time to know you're truly okay and will be there for them—unlike most other adults they have known.

Many older children who are newly adopted are on their best behavior when first adopted. Later, they may exhibit negative acting-out behavior—usually a test to see what you will do and whether you will still want them if they are bad. Testing you in this way may represent the child's attempt to bond with you. It may indicate that the child feels safe acting up with you and probably that he or she wants to keep *you*!

Are These Terms Used Too Loosely?

Some believe that bonding and attachment are used far too frequently and without much insight. "This overused word 'bonding' sometimes drives me wild," says Jean Nelson-Erichsen, LSW, M.A., assistant executive director of adoption at Los Niños International

Adoption in The Woodlands, Texas. "You don't usually just fall in love with people and become all warm and cuddly in days! And a lot of people whose babies are born to them don't immediately love their babies. The way you bond with children is to hold them and play with them and read to them. All the holding and caring things are important."

The downside of underlining the importance of bonding is that some mothers have suffered greatly because of their misguided beliefs about this issue. For example, some biological mothers who've had caesarean sections have believed that they couldn't bond because the child didn't have a vaginal birth. Other biological mothers thought they missed their chance at bonding because they were too ill after the birth to care for the child or the child was too ill to receive close contact. One adoptive mom took her son home from the hospital at the age of three days—and was told by others that it was too bad she couldn't bond to him but that it was too late! Fortunately, this level-headed mother scoffed at such nonsense.

Who Invented Bonding?

Where did the concept of bonding come from? Much of it appears to have evolved from studies of geese, goats, monkeys, and other animals. Some question that the idea of bonding in humans is a reasonable concept at all. In her book *Mother-Infant Bonding: A Scientific Fiction*, psychologist Diane Eyer challenges the existence of bonding. She refers to the physicians in the 1970s who observed that if goat kids were separated from their mothers for even five minutes, then the mothers would reject the kids. These doctors then extended the concept to human mothers.

Is animal behavior always analogous to human behavior? "I've been very interested in your description of animal studies and bonding," said Debra, an adoptive parent. "I think they are very important if you are adopting a goose or a goat." Of course, she was being facetious, but her point was well taken.

Studies of bonding between humans have also been conducted. For example, pediatricians have studied women who had close contact with their infants within hours of their birth and compared these mothers to women who did not have immediate close contact. The pediatricians extrapolated from this study that such bonding provided a uniquely special relationship to both parties, which would hold for the child's lifetime. However, researchers have not duplicated these results, and there seems to be no scientific basis for the hypothesis that mother and child must immediately bond or else be doomed to an unhappy relationship.

Nearly fifty years ago, researcher John Bowlby observed the behaviors and outcomes of children in orphanages who exhibited many problems and even death from the lack of care. Bowlby also compared the attachment of human infants to their mothers to the attachments between goslings and geese.

As a result of his observations, Bowlby developed a theory that early maternal influence was necessary to a child's health and stability. He apparently did not consider the negative factors found in numerous orphanages: the broad range of types of caregivers, the unsanitary conditions, and environments that differed extremely from a family home. In one orphanage, when maintenance of a clean facility and regular care of the infants was instituted, the result was a 17 percent drop in the death rate.

CAN ADOPTION INTERFERE
WITH BONDING AND ATTACHMENT?

Sometimes people worry that they won't be able to love a child that was not born to them—or that the child will not be able to love them. Some people presume that there is a uniquely special, almost mystical relationship between a biological mother and her child.

Yet, sadly, some biological parents abuse or neglect their children. Some people believe this behavior stems from a lack of bonding to the infant. But there is no proof that mothers who did not cuddle their newborn infants are more likely to abuse them.

Bonding continues to loom large as an issue to many physicians, nurses, and others. Many hospital staffers now pressure new mothers to hold their infants. The downside of this very heavy emphasis on bonding is that as mentioned earlier, some experts believe that if this psychological superglue process does not happen within a specific time frame (which varies a great deal, depending on the expert), then the child could later develop serious problems. Fortunately, many physicians believe that a parent-infant attachment can occur when the child is older than days, weeks, or even months.

SHOULD WE THROW OUT BONDING WITH THE BATH WATER?

Psychologist Diane Eyer thinks we should throw out concerns about bonding altogether: "There are many, many dimensions to the nurturance of our children. To the extent that we have reduced these processes to a 'bonding,' we have done ourselves a disservice. To the extent that we continue to deify the maternal-child relationship, hoping it will issue us transcendence from the mundane problems of an unpredictable world, we are lost."

Consider your own deeply held beliefs about bonding and attachment. If you truly believe that you will not be able to bond with a child who is not born to you, you could create a self-fulfilling prophecy. If you don't understand what all the fuss is about, you may be a good candidate to adopt. Of course, some doubt is understandable and reasonable, and many preadoptive parents have such doubts. But if your fear is very intense, then you should heed what your mind is telling you.

FATHERS AND BONDING

When discussing bonding and attachment, it's usually the mother-child interaction that is described; however, fathers can also bond.

Fathers are not usually the main nurturers and caregivers, but they still have special caring feelings for the child. Early on in infancy, the child recognizes the familiar faces of mother *and* father, and responds to their presence. Fathers are important to biological children and to adopted children.

WHAT KIND OF CHILD CAN YOU BOND WITH?

How can you know what type of child would fit best with your family? One way is to look at your own past relationships as indicators, particularly ones that did not last. For example, when a friendship or romantic relationship ended, what do you think was the cause? Was it because the other person was too clingy and you felt smothered— or was it because you wanted more attention and cuddling? Was the other person too irritable or so "up" all the time that you couldn't stand it?

Jot down a few reasons for your breakups with others, then think about what this might mean to you as a parent in the future. If you couldn't stand someone because you felt he or she was too demanding, then it might be a bad idea to adopt a child who has a medical problem that requires constant attention. On the other hand, if you love caring for others, you and that same child might form a great relationship.

Also, think about the positive relationships you've had. What were the things that held you together—personality traits, common interests, something else? Considering your happy friendships and relationships can also help you in self-evaluation.

If you are a very active person who loves constant change, you might have difficulty with the child whose first reaction to anything new is "I hate it." Of course, if you plan to adopt an infant or a child who is not yet born, you cannot know if the child will be pliable or stubborn, positive or negative. You may be able to gain some clues from the birthmother's observed or reported behavior, but children are not always like their biological parents. In addition, the birthmother may feel she is in a crisis and thus be very stressed—factors that may alter her normal behavior.

If you are thinking about adopting a child who is a few months old or older, you may be able to learn a great deal about basic temperament—whether the baby is fussy, calm, or a little of both. If you are adopting an older child, you may be able to observe the child's behavior in person or through viewing a video.

Sometimes orphanages will provide "character reports" on children. Dr. Jenista thinks these can provide important information to prospective parents to help them decide whether they and the child might easily form a strong attachment. She says, "I think the most valuable things from the medical reports are the comments from the person taking care of the child. Comments such as, 'Three years old, loves to sing songs and put her hair in hairstyles and rearrange all the food on the plate precisely before she eats it. But if a stranger walks into the room, she runs and hides and refuses to say anything unless coaxed with promises of candy.' To me, that is normal."

What Jenista does *not* find helpful are the reports that say the child is cheerful, delightful, smart, loves all foods, and sleeps well every night. She doesn't believe it, because a mix of positive and negative comments is far more realistic.

Another way to evaluate a child is through viewing a videotape of a child who is unaware of being recorded. Says Jenista, "If you see one child snatching his favorite truck from somebody else and walking away without a glance at the other child, that tells you one thing. Or the child who does the same thing, but then pats the other child on the head and offers him a different toy, that says something different."

Dr. Jenista says that what is most important is *your* reaction to the behavior. "You look at yourself and say, 'If this is the child's true behavior—and it probably is—could I stand it? If I don't like this behavior, would I be able to put the effort into modifying it, or would I look at it and be so horrified that I would withdraw from this child?' "

Try to avoid thinking of the child's behavior as being "good" or "bad," and don't look at your own reactions that way either. Deal with your true feelings.

Dr. Jenista and I agree that most adopted children and parents form strong close attachments to each other. She says it's somewhat comparable to arranged marriages. Most of them actually do work and develop into reciprocal relationships over time, just as the vast majorities of adoptions, for whatever reason, also work.

BONDING WITH YOUR ADOPTED CHILD

Is it the same or different from bonding with a child you birth? I have the perspective of being a parent of two children by birth and one child by adoption. I did not find the attachment any different. Some people have told me that a person can only attach to a biological child and that I must be in denial. To those doubters, I offer one very basic example to illustrate my point: My two older children were born to me and when they were infants, I never minded changing their diapers, no matter how dirty they were. But when I babysat anyone else's baby, and had to change that child's diaper, I always felt extremely nauseated—one step away from vomiting. After we adopted our third child, it was the same as with the first two—changing his diapers never bothered me at all. It wasn't just parenting experience—other babies' dirty diapers still made me sick. This reaction was a good illustration of true bonding that I developed for each child, whether born to me or adopted.

In the beginning of this chapter, I mentioned seeing a bonding take place between adoptive parents and their child. The baby that John and Carol planned to adopt was born a few weeks ahead of schedule, but their home study was not yet complete. Because of a strange Florida law, the baby could not immediately be placed with John and Carol, but the attorney could place the baby with anyone else he chose. He chose me. And John and Carol moved in with me and their newborn child for a few days until the approval came through. Carol was the primary caregiver.

Carol was scared and excited and ran the gamut of emotions. She asked me to show her how to feed the baby, change him, and wash him. I did so—always stepping back to let her take over. I saw her love and confidence escalate as she rocked and cared for her son. I saw this rather reserved person sing to him, say silly things to him, and tell him that she loved him. I saw a bonding occur.

BONDING AND BREAST-FEEDING

Breast-feeding is a guilt area for many new mothers, whether biological moms who cannot or choose not to breast-feed or adoptive mothers. (Interestingly, in the original research on bonding, the "bonded" mothers bottlefed their infants.)

Again, I believe that adoptive moms can form very strong attachments to their infants. It's likely that much of the connection between breast-feeding and bonding with an infant is a function of the holding and loving warmth between mother and child. I would like to note, however, that in some cases it is possible for adoptive mothers to breast-feed, at least partially. If you are interested in this option, La Leche League offers a pamphlet on nursing the adopted baby.

BONDING STAGES
FOR ADOPTIVE PARENTS

In their book *Mothers and Their Adopted Children: The Bonding Process*, authors Dorothy W. Smith, Ed.D., and Laurie Nehls Sherwen, Ph.D., divided up what they saw as the three stages of adoption and bonding: Time 1, when the mother engaged in activities before the child was placed; Time 2, when bonding activities at the immediate time of placement occurred; and Time 3, later bonding activities.

One bonding activity—the prospective mother fantasizing about her future child—occurs in Time 1, before the child enters the family. She also begins to prepare the baby's room, buy baby clothes, and so forth.

When the child is placed with the family (Time 2), Smith and Sherwen identified an "immediate and prolonged contact with infant/child," as well as the interaction and nurturing of both mother and father with the child. The authors also believe that at the time of "first contact" with the child, it is important that significant others be present; for example, the other parent or other family members or friends. It's a sort of validation.

Bonding activities that occur after the immediate first contact (Time 3) are touching and hugging the child, talking to the child (whether newborn baby or older child), and caring for the child. From the child's perspective, bonding activities in this stage (the only stage for which the authors identified the child's "part" in bonding) were such things as responding to the mother's nurturing and eliciting physiological responses from the mother. One simple example of how a child elicits a response: he or she smiles at the mother. Newborns don't immediately smile, but within months, the developmental milestone of the smile, and the responses to the child's smile from the mother, can occur.

ENTITLEMENT

Tied to the concept of bonding is entitlement—the feeling that you deserve to be a parent and you feel like the "real parent" to the child. If you don't feel entitled, then you may end up feeling guilty, feeling as if you took another person's child away, even though the adoption was done voluntarily and with the full consent of the birthparents.

Why might some people not feel entitled to a child? They may feel frightened or unworthy. They may secretly believe that if God wanted them to have a baby, he would have let them be pregnant. So how could they deserve this child? They may also think they are not as good as biological parents. These are all common but usually transient feelings that adoptive parents need to overcome.

Some people adopt children from other countries because they believe their feelings of entitlement would be greater with international adoption than with U.S. adoption. Why? They can ignore the fact that the child was born to a birthmother, because in many cases the foreign child was abandoned at an orphanage. But it's not a good idea to deny the existence of a birthmother, no matter where she is from.

Some adoptive parents think it is very "cute" that their five-year-old or six-year-old thinks he came from "the plane." Children need to know that they were born, like everyone else. So if you cannot accept the idea that the child had a biological mother, perhaps you should table your adoption decision.

If you feel entitled to your child, you can be a much better parent than if you are constantly worried about whether or not you are worthy, if you truly deserve this child, and if this child "feels" like your child. So how can you know if you will feel entitled to an adopted child?

One possible way is to ask yourself if you generally feel as if you deserve the good things that have happened to you. If you have a good job and a nice home, or if other positive aspects of your life are important to you, ask yourself, What percentage of this/these achievement(s) are the result of my actions? How much did I contribute to what is good in my life?

Then think about the problem areas of your life—a job that could be better, health problems that need to be resolved, or any other areas that need (and can be) improved. What percentage of the problem is your fault?

If you are at the extreme ends—for example, if you respond that zero percent of the good aspects of your life result from your actions, and 100 percent of your problems are caused by your faults as a human, then you have a problem. You are not giving yourself any credit at all, and yet you are blaming yourself completely for every problem. Conversely, do you take full credit for the good aspects and zero blame for the problems? No one is completely in control of his or her life, and we are all somewhat at fault for problem areas. Both responses are very unrealistic. Before choosing parenthood, you need to reevaluate yourself.

Keep in mind that a sense of entitlement toward the adopted child can sometimes be a problem because of negative societal attitudes toward adoption and the view of some people that adoption is a kind of "second best" form of parenthood. Adoptive parents need to be aware of this attitude but not to internalize it.

Entitlement is actively discussed in open adoption. Open adoption refers to the adoptive parents and birthparents having knowledge of each other, usually having met and sometimes maintaining an ongoing relationship. Critics of open adoption believe that the adoptive parents would feel *less* entitled to the child if they know who the birthparents are and especially if they have a continuing relationship with them. Proponents, however, assert that the feelings of entitlement are *greater* in such an adoption and that the adoptive parents are far more secure, overall. (See Chapter 16 for more information on open adoption.)

5

TALKING
WITH YOUR SPOUSE
ABOUT ADOPTION

Y ou probably have at least mentioned the subject of adoption to your spouse, but perhaps he or she did not really take you seriously. For example, Colleen told her husband of three years that she thought adoption was a beautiful way to bring a child into the family, and he responded, "I thought I was the child in the family." This flippant remark troubled Colleen and caused her to delay further discussion. Her husband may have had no idea that she was truly serious about this issue and perhaps thought she was making a passing and rather oblique remark. He may also have been unprepared to discuss such a serious subject then.

A better way to approach the subject with a spouse would be to first say that you need to talk about something that is important to you. Of course, avoid bringing the subject up when your spouse is in the middle of figuring out your income taxes or resolving some work crisis. Choose a calm time.

Keep in mind that even if your spouse does accept that you are serious about adopting a child, his or her first response might be a negative one. "I don't want to take on somebody else's problems," is what some people have reportedly said. Or "It's too expensive and takes too long to adopt." Or "I don't feel like I could really relate to a child that didn't have my genes." (These are only a few of the broad array of reactions that may occur.)

COMMITMENT OF BOTH PARENTS
IS NECESSARY

Although it's often true that one member of a couple has a more intense desire to adopt than the other, both adults should be committed to adopting a child *before* applying to an adoption agency or making an appointment to see an adoption attorney. You owe it to yourselves. But more important, you owe a true commitment to the child who might become yours. She or he deserves to be placed with parents who want a child very much.

Attorney Douglas Donnelly of Santa Barbara, California, says that if both spouses aren't eager to adopt, he won't represent them. It's all right if one is more intensely interested than the other, but *both* must wish to adopt.

How does Donnelly judge a couple's mutual interest? "I'm a trial attorney by training and we learn to judge people's veracity by their body language and what they say and how they say it. By talking to people, I can tell who is excited and is not—by what questions they ask, by how they respond to my questions, and by whether they look me in the eye or stare at their shoes when they're talking." If he feels both spouses are not committed, he recommends they seek counseling and come back in a year or so. Donnelly became an adoption attorney after he and his wife adopted their two children.

Also keep in mind that if you have adopted one child and are considering adopting another, your spouse may not always agree with you the second time around, and again you will need to come to an agreement together. Those who have adopted for a second time say that it's not as stressful a process. "There wasn't the sense of panic and hopelessness the second time," said Tom. He knew what to expect and felt confident that he and his wife would succeed at adoption. And they did.

IF YOUR SPOUSE IS ENTHUSIASTIC

It's wonderful if you both agree that you want to adopt a child, but there still may be other issues to address. For example, you may wish to adopt an infant and your spouse may want an older child. You may want to adopt a child of another race and your spouse may insist on a same-race adoption. David believed that he could adopt a child with any medical problem, but his wife Jennifer wanted to adopt only a child who could live independently as an adult.

So even when you get beyond the if, keep in mind that there is a broad array of important issues to explore. Be open with each other.

IF YOUR SPOUSE IS UNCERTAIN

What if your spouse is not totally opposed to the idea of adopting a child but feels very unsure about it? This is actually a very reasonable reaction. Try to find out why your spouse is not sure about adoption. Maybe your partner needs information and education. Perhaps a visit to an adoptive parent group and the chance to meet adoptive parents could help ease concerns he or she might have. (And it would also help educate and inspire the person who is eager to adopt.)

Many adoption agencies have free orientation meetings that you can attend to learn about adopting through their agency. You can learn about policies, fees, and other areas of interest, and you can also ask questions. The agency may invite guest speakers or may show videotapes of talks by adoptive parents, birthparents, or even adopted adults.

Maybe your spouse still has unresolved feelings about infertility and would really rather pursue a pregnancy than to adopt a child. Or maybe he or she is concerned about the many adoption myths and fears (see Chapter 1).

IF YOUR SPOUSE IS VERY OPPOSED

If your spouse is firmly opposed to adoption and no amount of talking, cajoling, education, or other means you've tried work, then you will need to learn how to accept this fact. You may feel anger, resentment, disappointment, and other emotions, but you will need to refocus on your relationship as marital partners and either return to attempts to create a biological child or give up the dream of parenthood.

This situation is not an easy one. Counseling may be necessary for the person who wanted to adopt so fervently. But it's important to remember that the spouse is not a bad person because he or she is opposed to adoption.

Sometimes an infertile person is opposed to adoption. He or she believes that just one more treatment or one more doctor might make the miracle of conception happen, and that agreeing to adopt would be tantamount to giving up.

You may find it very difficult to accept your spouse's decision not to adopt. It is an emotionally charged issue that can affect your relationship, but it may help to remember that if your spouse is not eager to adopt, then your home would not be the best place for a child. You may need to go through a grieving process as well, as you give up your dreamchild.

This may sound painful or unthinkable to the person who longs to adopt—but there are many people who do not have children and who have good marriages and very successful relationships with others. Some of them work with children, in their jobs or in volunteer efforts, or they find fulfillment in other ways.

COPING WITH THE DRAGGER/ DRAGGEE PROBLEM

Some social workers refer to the common problem of spouses disagreeing about whether they should adopt a child as the "dragger/ draggee syndrome." It's a facetious-sounding (and yes, pretty negative) phrase, but it's easy to guess that the one who wishes to adopt is the dragger and the one who is reluctant is the draggee. Sometimes spouses switch roles midstream, and the dragger becomes the draggee and vice versa.

Do not assume that most of the draggers are women. Clinical psychologist C. Michael Snyter of Glenside, Pennsylvania, who counsels preadoptive couples, says that although most people assume that women are ready to adopt and that men are reluctant, he has seen plenty of both cases.

Consider how deeply felt is your need for a biological child. Also consider how intense your desire to become a parent is. If you can't have a biological child with your partner, will you feel truly deprived? Because if you believe or feel that you are cheated in life by your partner's infertility (or by your own), you might need to focus on the marriage itself and think about what are the important issues in life for you. Who comes first in your life?

Some couples reason that they need their child to have at least "half" their genes, and for them, donor insemination or surrogate motherhood are the best answers if pregnancy cannot be achieved otherwise.

Spouses should share their feelings with each other, while taking into account that these are very emotional issues. Your spouse may feel guilty that he or she is infertile. Or your spouse may feel sad or even angry that you are infertile. You may think your spouse already knows how you feel, but it's amazing how many misunderstandings and hurts can continue because of a lack of communication.

When you both get your feelings "on the table," it can ease a lot of the unspoken issues as well as the pain, and can also help you work together toward making the decision about whether or not you two should adopt a child.

As the goal of adoption becomes closer, the reluctant person may begin to see adopting as much more positive and the former dragger may start to panic as reality sets in. If this happens to you, it does not mean that you should withdraw your application to the agency. What it means is that your gut-level, innermost computer is telling you to step back and think about this decision a little more.

The doubter has not really changed his or her mind. (Usually.) But as the adoption prospect looms closer, she or he may be scared and doubtful about being a good parent. (Psychologists call this an approach-avoidance conflict. The further away you are from a goal, the more appealing it seems. The closer you get, the more uncertain you are about the goal.) The prospective adoptive parent needs to try to determine the basis for the sudden hesitation and fear. Both partners need to decide together how they should deal with this.

It may help to emphasize here that rarely are both husband and wife in exact sync about how much (or if) they want to adopt. Almost invariably, one person's desire to adopt is stronger than the other's, even if the degree of difference is small. The main point to keep in mind is that before you actually take steps to adopt a child, you need a strong mutual commitment. This is important for you and very important for your child, if you adopt.

6

INFERTILITY ISSUES
IN ADOPTION

Some couples have extreme difficulty deciding if and when the quest for a biological child should end. Others, at some point, just become sick of the whole fertility treatment process and decide that what they really want is a child, and they adopt. Pregnancy and birth no longer seem paramount. Others decide that children will not be in their future, and they work to accept this. They do not wish to adopt, for a variety of reasons.

This chapter discusses how people feel about infertility and how they feel about adoption. Sometimes men and women share common feelings, but sometimes their emotions are very different.

EXTERNAL FACTORS TO CONSIDER

In deciding whether to continue with fertility treatments or to consider adoption, some couples look at the odds of success. For example, they presume that the chance for a baby might be x percent in another fertility procedure, whereas they may see the chance for a baby with an agency or attorney is nearly 100 percent. So if the percentages influence them (and also if they have already invested heavily, both financially and emotionally, in infertility testing but with no success), they may switch gears to adoption. Or they may end the quest for children altogether.

Still others give up their attempts at conception when the insurance money is gone and their own personal financial resources are exhausted. In those cases, they may have to delay adoption because they cannot afford adoption fees; however, with the new federal adoption tax credit and employer adoption benefits, adoption may at last be feasible for many more families.

Another issue for some couples is secondary infertility, which refers to couples who have one or more birth children but who can no longer have children yet they want more children. These couples receive very little sympathy—and sometimes quite a bit of antagonism—from people with a "primary" infertility. The important thing to keep in mind is to do what's best for your family.

One key step in deciding whether or not you truly wish to adopt is to consider your innermost feelings, not just about adoption but about your infertility—your own or as a couple—and how those feelings affect your attitude toward yourself.

THE DECISION-MAKING PROCESS FOR INFERTILE COUPLES

As you move along in your evaluation of whether you will ultimately become a parent through adoption, and, if so, how you'll achieve that goal, most of you who are infertile will eventually settle into one of five distinct decision-making paths:

1. You'll decide to adopt, and you'll abandon infertility treatments, sometimes with great relief.
2. You will decide to adopt and give up infertility treatments for now. Maybe later you will revisit infertility treatments and seek to bear a biological child as well.
3. You decide you will not adopt and instead that you will continue with infertility treatment.
4. You decide not to adopt and not to continue with infertility treatments. You will not become a parent.
5. You stop infertility treatment for now. You don't consciously decide that you won't adopt, but you don't pursue adoption. Perhaps later you will revisit adoption or infertility treatment.

COMMON EMOTIONS ASSOCIATED WITH INFERTILITY

As you consider whether or not you should adopt a child, you can expect to experience a flood of different and sometimes conflicting emotions. It's almost inevitable that some of these emotions are negative, such as anger, frustration, impatience, and general feelings of hopelessness. However, it is often helpful to understand that many other people experience these same emotions and that you are not alone if you feel this way, too.

Denial

A very common reaction for most people who learn of their infertility is to deny that it can be true. (Denial is commonly a first reaction to major traumatic events of life.) The doctor must have made a mistake. Someone mixed up the lab results. Something else happened. You don't believe it.

Then, after the initial denial and shock are over, many people become very angry. In fact, some people are still extremely angry about their infertility when they apply to adopt a child. If you are enraged about your infertility, wait a while before you consider adoption. You need time to accept your situation before moving on to a different path.

Anger at Infertility in General

Anger is one of the most common emotions because infertility seems so unfair. In a way, it's a healthy emotion, because although anger is no fun, it can eventually enable you to deal with the grief and loss connected to your inability to have a biological child. Of course, it's possible to get "stuck" in anger, and that can be difficult for you, your spouse, your friends, and your relatives. Tell them that you are not mad at them, so they won't worry needlessly that they may have offended you.

Adoption agencies report that many adopting couples are very angry, not only about the unfairness of their infertility but also about the many requirements they must undergo as prospective adoptive parents. They really hate the idea that they must prove their worthiness while people they perceive as incompetent parents can bear child after child, with no one asking them for references, no one making them undergo a physical examination or talking with a social worker or taking classes, and so forth.

Maxine Chalker, executive director of Adoptions From the Heart, in Ardmore, Pennsylvania, used to teach night courses for preadoptive couples. She encountered such rage and hostility when she talked about birthparents that she was shocked. "I think they're mad at the fact that they have to go anywhere to ask for a child, and can't have one like other people. I think there is about equal levels of anger between men and women, and the angry ones are very argumentative. They want to know, 'Why do we have to do this, why do we have to do that, I don't think this is fair, why does this cost so much?' and so forth. The angry people are aggressive and hostile, which is strange because they are coming to our agency for what they ultimately want and no one could give them—a child!"

Many of these preadoptive couples needed to work on resolving their own grief and anger about their infertility—before ever considering adoption. After all, if you continue to feel anger or contempt toward a woman whose child you adopted, how will this translate in the future when you explain adoption to your child? How might it affect how you feel about any negative traits your child may display? Will you blame all the "problem" behavior on his birthparents? Children who think their biological parents were bad will wonder if they are bad, too. It's important to consider your feelings about the infertility and if you are truly ready to adopt a child. You will probably never be happy about being infertile or stop wondering what it might be like to have a biological child. But you need to work on eliminating the rage and anger.

Shock and Powerlessness

Many people who delayed attempts at childbearing until their early thirties or later have been flabbergasted to learn that they have a problem conceiving a child. They may believe that if you try hard enough, you will succeed. So they try very hard. But sometimes, no matter what you do, a pregnancy does not happen. And this is very difficult to accept.

Infertile people often feel that they have been thwarted by their own bodies. They may also feel cheated. Marriage and family are part of the American Dream. They have the marriage and, for whatever reason, they do not have the children. One social worker told me that some people behave as if they half seriously think that having children is something guaranteed in the Bill of Rights—the "right to have children" (along with the right to bear arms, etc.). It's understandable that they feel this way. Having children is an accepted part of life—

something in the background—until you have problems conceiving. Yet sometimes, no matter how much money and time are expended, the pregnancy does not occur.

Feelings of Inadequacy

Because of the inability to conceive, both men and women can suffer feelings of inadequacy. Some women say that they feel they are defective and maybe don't even deserve a child. They may feel unfeminine and unattractive. Men may feel inadequate, in the sense both of having a defective body and of not being able to give their wives what they want most.

BIOLOGICAL PARENTHOOD VS. ADOPTION

In a 1995 issue of *Research in Nursing & Health*, professor Margarete Sandelowski, Ph.D., RN, described her findings based on her research with infertile couples, some of whom adopted children. She also compared the couples to fertile couples. According to Sandelowski, four main stages in the parenthood process affect both new biological parents and new adoptive parents: redefining nature in terms of biological parenthood and its importance; holding back/ letting go; claiming and caring for the fetus and/or child; assuming the identity of a parent.

Sandelowski saw "redefining nature" as a very difficult task for infertile couples. Couples considering adoption had to rethink adoption as an acceptable alternative to biological parenthood. The holding back/letting go process is hard. It means accepting that adoption (or assisted conception) is positive to you.

In the third process of claiming and caring for the fetus or child, biological parents (who were formerly infertile couples) used the prenatal period to think about the baby, talk about it, and so forth. After birth, they actively interacted with the new baby. Many prospective adoptive parents reported thinking about the child who would be coming into their lives, particularly if they had some concrete validation that the adoption was "real," such as a photograph or videotape of the child they would adopt. Many people have told me that they bonded to a child's photograph, and I believe them.

The "parental identity" stage involved couples actually perceiving themselves as parents. In this stage, most couples find themselves becoming extremely involved in child care as well as thinking about the baby. Said the author, "Couples reported feeling fully parental after 'immersing' themselves in the caretaking of their children and after 'being initiated' into parenthood by their baby's colic or illness."

Added Sandelowski, "Adopting couples, in particular, anticipated feeling fully parental only after they had been with their child longer than its birth or foster parents or after final adoption papers were processed." You too may find yourself a little fearful at giving total love to your new child, because you may worry about something going wrong and the adoption not being finalized. However, in my opinion, very few people are able to dam up their love for a new child, particularly an infant.

SECONDARY INFERTILITY: MAJOR ISSUES

If you have one or more biological children and would like more but you know you cannot have more children, then you have what is called "secondary infertility." (People who have never had children and are unable to conceive have "primary infertility.") Expect very little sympathy from most people with a primary infertility problem. In fact, some people with secondary infertility have found themselves personally attacked at infertility support meetings or group sessions, because those with primary infertility think that those with secondary infertility should be grateful and happy that they have at least one child already.

Yet it is very painful to have a secondary infertility. Those who try to deny people with this problem the right to grieve their loss and their attempts to create a pregnancy or to adopt a child make the whole situation even more painful. Some people believe that by virtue of having borne one or more children, the shock of secondary infertility is even greater, particularly when no cause can be identified.

If you or someone you know faces this issue, you may wish to ask your local RESOLVE group if they have special groups or sessions for people with secondary infertility or if they could recommend people for you to talk with. (See Appendix B for a list of RESOLVE groups.) You could also read *Wanting Another Child: Coping with Secondary Infertility* by Harriet Fishman Simon.

MEN'S AND WOMEN'S REACTIONS TO INFERTILITY AND ADOPTION

Although men and women do share many common emotions about infertility and adoption, they also have distinctive differences in how they react and in how they cope.

Researchers have found that women and men have very different coping styles in dealing with infertility. One study of sixteen middle-class people (eight couples) seeking a pregnancy revealed that women were far more verbal than were men in coping with the problem. In fact, the men were uncomfortable talking about the problem. Their response was to try to work toward problem solving— when in most cases the women were primarily seeking an opportunity to discuss their feelings. Some men are more expressive than others, but some can talk about their feelings only with their wives or their male friends.

This study did not include adoption, but if one can extrapolate, it seems likely that when women are considering adoption, they are more likely to talk about the issue frequently, both before deciding and during the process of the adoption itself.

The study also revealed that although both men and women were unhappy with the health care system, men were especially negative, feeling that the system was paternalistic and uncaring and made them feel helpless. In considering the adoption system, it is possible that men may also feel very powerless—especially since the adoption system is a "maternal" system run mostly by females.

If you're a woman, try to realize that your partner's unwillingness to discuss the problem doesn't mean he doesn't care about it. And if you're a man, try to understand that your partner needs a chance to express her feelings and gain your empathy—listening and empathizing would be greatly appreciated.

Women: Experiencing Anger at Other Moms

"When I was undergoing fertility treatments, I avoided going to the supermarket when I thought mothers with children would be there," said Lorna. (She is now an adoptive parent who goes to the market whenever she feels like it.) "I'd go after ten at night or early in the morning." But sometimes, despite her best efforts to avoid the sight of children, Lorna would see women with children anyway, and she would feel angry and empty. Many infertile women report feeling this way. Unfortunately, enforced self-isolation can lead to increased distress and loneliness for the infertile woman.

An infertile woman can feel anger and jealousy when friends, relatives, and coworkers become pregnant and when she is invited to baby showers. The infertile woman who believes everyone in the world can have a baby except her can experience a lot of pain. Infertility seems to hit women especially hard, whether the infertility is theirs or their spouse's. This is probably because only women can become pregnant.

Interestingly, few males report anger at seeing children or pregnant women, despite their own intense desire to have a child. This is probably one of the many gender differences in response to infertility. Many infertile men yearn for children as much as women do, but the manner in which they react and express their emotions is often very different.

Women: Feeling Anger at Their Menstrual Period

When an infertile woman is seeking to conceive a child, she may feel anger or even despair when her menstrual cycle starts again. It's the last thing she wants. Or maybe her period is a few days late and she thinks, "Could this be IT!? Finally?" And then she starts menstruating. Crash. Angry about the "failure" again, she seems to see even more pregnant women everywhere. (It's amazing how all those pregnant women disappear after a family has a child through pregnancy or adoption.)

Joanie never knew why she was infertile. She just knew she still wanted a baby, and she admitted that until she actually went through menopause, each month she hoped that her period would not occur— and that she might be pregnant. And she felt this way even after she had happily adopted several children. Joanie was a good mother and she loved her children, but she still had that tiny little hope in the back of her mind that she could have a biological child.

Experts differ on whether infertility must be entirely "resolved" before adoption, but most of the people I interviewed, experts and adoptive parents alike, agreed that a sadness over infertility may not ever go away entirely. But the person who seeks to adopt should not be in an active grieving period.

Men and Infertility

Most studies center on women and their feelings toward infertility, but one interesting study of three hundred infertile males was reported in a 1988 issue of *Psychology Today*. Some of the men decided to remain childless, whereas others adopted; and the researchers found distinctive differences between the adopters and the non-adopters.

For example, about one-fourth of the men dealt with their infertility by involving themselves in activities with other people's children, such as coaching a baseball team or working with a church group. Others became self-involved with body building or health issues. The largest group substituted a nonhuman object to pay attention to, such as a house or a car.

None of the men who elected for a self-centered choice decided to adopt, and only a few who used objects as substitutes became adoptive fathers. But over half of the men who became involved with the children of others chose to adopt. Of all three groups, this group was also the most successful in their marriages. Said the author, "We believe that men who are experiencing infertility should take a good close look at the way they are dealing with the issue. Their choices could be something they have to live with for a very long time."

This does not mean that a woman whose husband suddenly decides to join a gym should abandon all hope at adopting a child, especially in today's era of encouraging fitness. But if he also seems generally disinterested in children, ignores them when he is around them, and obsesses about his own health, he might not be ready to be a father.

Men's Feelings About Their Family Name and Adoption

Although many women continue to use their maiden name when they marry, or they hyphenate their maiden name with that of their husband's, most women take their husband's last name when they marry.

As a result, "carrying on the family name" is usually seen as a male responsibility. If a man perceives this to be important, it can directly affect the adoption decision.

Why? Because he may see it as wrong to "give" the family name to a nonbiological child. And even if he does not see it this way, it's likely that other family members will. Of course, circumstances vary. For example, if this will be the very first grandchild in the extended family, the grandparents may be very disapproving about conferring the family name on an adopted child. On the other hand, if there are many grandchildren in the family, the extended family may not care so much about carrying on the family name.

Worrying so much about the family name may sound strange or elitist to some of us, particularly those of us who are female, but it is clearly a real constraint for some people considering adoption. Said Sherrod in her 1995 article on male perspectives on infertility, "The concept of immortality, characterized as the ability to continue the bloodline or carry on the family name, emerged as a major theme." Conversely, Sherrod found that women identified primarily with the motherhood aspect of having a child, rather than with immortality and the family name issue.

Men's Sexuality, Fertility, and Adoption

"He's shooting blanks!" is one comment directed against men who are infertile. Some men who find out that a couple is actively seeking a pregnancy think it's hilariously funny to ask the husband if he needs any "help." (Nudge, nudge, wink, wink.) But such remarks are not at all humorous to most men. A man's image of virility may be threatened, and he doesn't like it. He may think that a "real man" can conceive a child and that his low (or no) sperm count or other problems indicate that he is less than a real man. The problem can sometimes affect him sexually, until he realizes that even if he can't reproduce, he's still a sexual being.

Of course, women can feel inadequate as well when they don't achieve a pregnancy, but it's a different kind of inadequacy, related more to feminine identity than to sexual abilities. People do not make jokes about dropping "blank eggs," for example. If anything, the infertile female receives far more sympathy for her plight than does the infertile male—and yet male infertility is no more under the control of the man than female infertility is under the control of the woman.

Another problem for infertile men while they're "trying" to have a child is that they must often provide sex on demand, when the wife is most fertile. Some men say they feel like a sex machine, with all the fun and spontaneity taken out of it. Most women don't like the "mechanization" of sex, but they maintain the attitude that if that's what it takes, then we'll do it.

The attitude of insensitive others does not help much either—especially others who ask whose "fault" the infertility is. I don't see any reason why anyone but your doctor needs that information. In fact, it might be a good idea to mention here that most people find it very hard to deal with the probing questions of others when they are seeking to create a pregnancy or when they are trying to adopt a child. If you find people repeatedly asking you questions that you prefer not to answer, you can feign deafness. Or you could say to the other person, unsmilingly, "Why do you want to know?" This generally deflects nosy questions.

Even today, a man's identity is often socially and culturally linked with his work identity, and thus it may be harder for a man to express his desire to become a parent. In the past, many people thought "house husbands" would become commonplace—but that has not happened, and it is probably directly related to the male work identity.

A Lack of Control Is Considered "Unmasculine"

Although both males and females experience feelings of powerlessness with infertility (and also often with adoption), it appears to be a bigger problem for men, probably because many men are reared to be take-charge people. When they find that they have a fertility problem, the control is gone. To cope with the emotional pain, many men resort to denying that they have a problem, rationalizing that everything will be all right, and absorbing themselves heavily in activities such as work or recreation.

In contrast, women who are distressed by their infertility find it difficult to accelerate their level of activities or even to maintain their normal lifestyle in many cases, and they are more likely to turn inward with their emotional pain.

A man may feel that he is asserting himself and reclaiming his control over the situation by saying that if he cannot have a biological child, then he doesn't want a child at all, thus feeling that the control is returned to him. He may remain adamant in this position—or he may change his mind later. If the woman strongly wishes to adopt, however, she may feel that her own control over their life together is taken away, that her feelings are not important to the man, and a variety of other emotions.

On the other hand, a man may conclude that adoption will enable him to regain control of the problem once again. Consequently, he may think that adoption is a good way to become a parent. And it may be the wife who is the person who is reluctant to adopt.

A FEMALE-CENTERED
ADOPTION WORLD

Most studies and literature on reactions toward infertility and adoption focus on women rather than on men. This may be because of the biological nature of pregnancy, and thus is more understandable in an infertile couple trying to achieve pregnancy. But men's attitudes are important—and are probably ignored far too often.

Most adoption agencies are staffed by female social workers who may not empathize with the feelings, fears, and concerns of men and are far more likely to concentrate on the female prospective parent. Another possible reason why men may be somewhat shortchanged in considering their needs is that often it is assumed that females will manage all or most parenting tasks—which is not always true.

In fact, several years ago, shortly after an unexpected illness claimed the life of an adoptive mother, an adoption agency sought the return of the child from the bereaved and shocked adoptive father. He fought back in court and prevailed in retaining custody of his daughter.

Men who are uncomfortable discussing their emotions openly may find some infertility and preadoptive counseling groups unsuitable. Some women have also told me they felt very nervous talking about their feelings in a group and that they preferred to talk to a close friend or a therapist instead.

Rather than a one-size-fits-all approach to infertility and the adoption decision, it would be far more helpful if counselors and social workers tailored their approaches to the individual—whether male or female. For instance, a man who does not talk about his infertility but instead begins working on special projects may have found a perfectly valid way to resolve his emotions. Remember the study that indicated that infertile men who became very involved in activities with children were more likely to eventually become parents.

BE PATIENT WITH EACH OTHER

Both sexes need to understand that men and women may react differently to infertility and to adoption and they need to cultivate patience with each other. Women need to understand that most men do not talk about infertility publicly and instead tend to repress their feelings or sublimate them by engaging in other activities.

Men need to understand that women may see pregnancy as an achievement and infertility as a personal failure. Men should also encourage their partners to seek out supportive groups or caring friends and family members who can talk with them about the problem. And men themselves should be able to find a close friend or relative to privately share frustrations and anxieties with—whether the issue is infertility or adoption—or both.

MEN, WOMEN, AND THE BOTTOM LINE

Whether it's fertility treatment or adoption that is being considered, there are most definitely costs to consider. Some of the men and women I interviewed told me that they saw adoption as more of a sure thing, because they believed if they paid adoption fees, they would eventually become parents, whereas if they paid fertility fees, they had no guarantees at all. Some saw fertility treatment payments as a kind of "black hole" that could gobble up all their savings.

It seemed to me that men were more concerned about long-term expenses. For example, some women worried about adoption fees or fertility expenses but did not look at the overall long-term cost of rearing a child; whereas men considered the expense of children over the course of at least twenty years. As a result, one of the issues that came up sometimes when women wanted to adopt and men did not, was that men felt it was too costly from a long-range perspective, particularly when a second child was being considered.

In addition, it seemed to me that men worried more than women about being "too old" to adopt. For example, Don, age forty-two, computed that if he adopted right away, he'd still be over age sixty when his child would graduate from high school. The thought of putting a child through college in his retirement years frightened him.

Many women, however, seem more concerned with their urgent desire to have a child now, rather than concentrating on the future, years down the road.

This analysis may sound sexist to you, and your situation may be quite different. These are overall patterns, and everyone does not fit. Yet, despite many good changes in our society, there are and always will be some male and female differences. I think it's better to acknowledge them when they do exist and to accept them rather than to try to pretend that we are all androgynously alike.

If we can accept and understand our differences, as well as what makes us similar, those who decide to become adoptive parents will be far more effective at parenting. Whether you adopt a boy or girl (if you do adopt), if you can accept gender differences while still challenging your children to do their best and loving them unconditionally, you will be a more flexible and better parent.

7

HOW IMPORTANT
IS BIOLOGY?

Are you who you are because you're Tom and Alice's son or daughter? Or because you worked hard in school, overcame many obstacles, made a few mistakes along the way as well—and now, here you are? In other words, are you who you are mostly because of "nature" (your genetic heritage) or because of "nurture"? (your environment). Or because of both?

This is not just an interesting rhetorical question—it is a valid issue to consider. If you think that you've become the person you are primarily because of the great (or not-so-great) genes that you've inherited, then you probably set a high store on the importance of heredity and tend to devalue the impact of environmental influences. But if you think you are "you" primarily because of what has happened to you during your life, then you set a high value on the importance of environment. In that case, you may think that a good family is all a kid needs to turn out okay.

Many people, if they think about the nature/nurture issue at all, figure it's probably a combination of the two that makes a person what he or she is, and that most of the time, it's too hard to figure out what gene or what experience caused what outcome. I share this opinion.

So why did I include a chapter on the importance of biology? Because many people *do* consider genetics to be important, and because when you adopt a child, you are obviously adopting an individual with a very different set of genes from yours. Today, many physicians and researchers seem to think that many medical problems are probably (or will be) traceable to a person's genetic background.

The issue of genetics may also be a factor in your decision whether to adopt. There is general disagreement between adoptive parents and adoption professionals about whether genetic issues are important to adopting parents, as well as about *how* important they may be. A study published in the *British Journal of Psychology* in 1993 revealed that two groups, adoptive parents and other adults (not adopted adults) who did not know about a genetic parent's background were more likely to think that heredity was strongly important than did biological parents or children who grew up with both biological parents.

You need to determine if the genetics issue is important to you, because your opinion will influence not only whether you adopt but what kind of child you adopt.

GENETIC PREFERENCES AND PREDISPOSITIONS DO EXIST

Numerous research studies claim that some behaviors and preferences are related to our genes. For example, one study of twins raised apart from each other revealed that both twins had strong preferences for orange juice, chicken, sweetened cereal, and other specific food items. Of course, heredity is NOT all, and the environment in which a person is raised is clearly important to one's life. For example, one study showed the importance of genetics in obesity; another revealed that although genes were important, the person's *environment* also had a direct result on the body mass of an adopted person. The study compared adult adoptees to their birthparents, adoptive parents, and biological full and half-siblings.

AN ADOPTED CHILD MAY OR MAY NOT LOOK OR BE LIKE YOU

At an adoption picnic several years ago, I was sitting with my husband and my son. One woman at our table kept rattling on and on about the importance of children resembling their parents. (Why she was at an adoption picnic is a mystery I never solved.) At one point, she pointed to my son and then to me and my husband and said, "For example, it's perfectly obvious that this boy is yours—he looks just like your husband!" I responded by saying, "Really! And he was adopted, too!"

What often happens is that children pick up on the behavior, mannerisms, and even the type of language their parents use. This may then give them a "resemblance" that others see immediately—as did the woman at the picnic.

It's perfectly okay to feel that your adopted child is like you or even that he or she looks like you—whether it's true or not. Studies done in England by social worker Lois Raynor revealed that the happiest adoptive parents and adopted children were those who thought they were like each other—even when no one else could see it. They believed they were alike in looks or temperament or interests or some other aspect. When you think about it, almost any two people have something that can be found in common.

It's important to keep in mind—and this is hard—that if you had a biological child, that child would not necessarily resemble you or your spouse. In fact, you and your spouse could be quiet intellectuals, and your child could be very extroverted and athletic and care little for books.

One advantage of adoptive parenting is that many adoptive parents presume that the child will probably *not* be a lot like them, and they accept this. As a result, there is a much lower probability that the child will feel forced into certain interests or career choices. (It's interesting, however, that many adopted sons follow in the career paths of their adoptive fathers. We don't know if this is true for females as well.) You need to imagine yourself being open to helping your child explore the many different aspects of life to learn where his or her interests and talents lie.

Many studies indicate that most children adopted as infants grow up to be healthy and well-adjusted people. They may, however, be very unlike their adoptive parents. Some scientists believe that temperaments are inherent and that even the newborn may be naturally fussy or essentially contented and blasé about life.

Sometimes even biological parents find it difficult to adapt to a child whose temperament differs greatly from their own. Psychiatrists Stella Chess and Alexander Thomas have studied the aspect of temperament for nearly forty years and found that parents may need to adapt their own parenting styles to a child's very different temperament to attain a "goodness of fit" between parent and child. If parents can accept and adapt to a child's temperamental style and also help the child accept and adapt, life is a lot easier for everyone involved. (This does *not* mean that parents are told to indulge the child's every whim.)

Accepting basic differences in temperament can give adoptive parents a kind of head start over the many biological parents who continue to expect their children to be clones of themselves, and who, by this expectation, doom themselves and their children to constant exasperation or worse.

PREDISPOSITIONS: THEY ARE GOOD, BAD, AND NEUTRAL

Having a "genetic predisposition" means that you carry a gene for a particular trait—one that may or may not "come out," depending on your environmental factors. It is thought that some mental illnesses are heavily based on genetic predispositions. For example, schizophrenia, a severe mental illness in which the person is detached from reality, is paranoid, hallucinates, and exhibits other unsettling symptoms, may be genetically based. But many people also believe that the illness may not be triggered unless some other factor occurs, such as severe stress or a viral illness.

Of course, there are many positive genetic predispositions, such as athletic ability, musical or artistic talent, and so forth. Or neutral ones such as eye color (unless you think one eye color is "better" than another).

The point I'm trying to make here is that we all have genetic predispositions to "good" and "bad" traits, and adopted children have these genetic propensities as well. If you place a very strong emphasis on the importance of genes, then you are likely to look for certain things to happen. For example, if you think genetic predispositions are critically important and if you know that your adopted child's birthfather had a problem with alcoholism, then you may have a strong fear that the child could grow up to become an alcoholic.

Lucie is an adoptive mother who told me that she constantly warns her son that he must never ever take a drink because he could become an alcoholic, just like his father. If this child ever does drink, is it inevitable that he would become an alcoholic? I do not think so. The probability is there, but it is *not* an inevitability. Take care that your belief does not become a self-fulfilling prophecy. When you are told that you cannot or should not do something, you often want to do it—it's the forbidden fruit syndrome. So if the child who was told he must never let alcohol pass his lips does actually take a drink, and if he does become an alcoholic, what impact could his mother's constant warnings over the years have had?

If you believe that certain genetic predispositions are critically important or dangerous, then you should not adopt a child whose family appears to have those background traits. Or perhaps you should not adopt at all. Virtually every family has someone who is an alcoholic or someone who has major depression or another problem. What about Aunt Mary, who never left her house because she was "eccentric"? Think about it. Your family members probably have a few problems, too.

Think about your family's medical problems. Perhaps your mother or father has high blood pressure. Both of my parents have high blood pressure, so one would think that I would have this problem, too. The predisposition would certainly seem to be there. But I don't have high blood pressure and never have had it.

An adopted child's birth family may have medical problems that he or she may or may not develop. Again, no guarantees. "I think people become extremely fired up about getting all the medical information," says Jean Erichsen of Los Niños International Adoption. "But the point is, it's not the medical problem that's going to do them in—it's really behavioral problems or their ability to adjust to the child and to help modify the child's behavior so that family life is harmonious." She adds, "Don't expect perfection—know that with adoption, you will have to make compromises. How much of life is exactly the way you anticipate—not much! Whether it's your job, your spouse, your house, or something else."

Think about your own views about heredity and environment and consider how important each is in your worldview and how important they are interactively. Think about how this affects your decision to adopt.

HOW IMPORTANT IS HEREDITY TO YOU?

To help you determine how significant the issue of heredity versus environment is to your life, consider your responses to the following questions. There are no right or wrong answers. If you believe that heredity is very important, then you will need to think about whether or not you can accept an adopted child who shares none of your genes. On the other hand, if you think environment is paramount, can you accept it if the child grows up to be very different from your expectations for him or her?

1. Someone you know has a problem such as attention deficit disorder or a learning disability. Is your first reaction to think that she or he must have "bad genes"? If so, do you think such problems can be overcome? Ask yourself how you might feel if a child you adopted had similar problems.

   Conversely, if someone you know wins first place in an athletic competition, do you think it's because he or she comes from a family of athletes? Or is it because of the heavy training that he or she endured?

2. Do you believe that children are primarily molded and shaped by their environment? Ask yourself how you would feel if you adopted a child and that child turned out to be very different from what you had envisioned (not bad or good—just different).

3. At your next meeting with relatives, notice how often (or if) they mention genetics. "He's just like his father!" or "Sandy loves those jalapeño peppers! She's got a cast-iron stomach, just like her mother." Are these comments mostly playful and innocuous? Does being like or looking like your relatives seem to be a big issue in your family? More important, is it a big issue for you?

4. If a parent has musical or artistic ability, do you assume that his or her children will also have these abilities? What if they don't?

5. Do you think that good parents almost always have children who are successful in life?

6. If a child is older than an infant when placed for adoption, will the child's previous life have any effect on his or her life after adoption? Why or why not?

7. Quick! Which is more important, heredity or environment? Don't think, just respond.

8

SINGLE ADOPTIVE
PARENTS

M any people believe that only married couples should adopt children, and most placing organizations continue to believe that a two-parent family is best for children. Some think that it's too difficult for a single person to parent a child today, but single people *are* adopting.

Although still a minority (no statistics exist on how many adopters are single), there is a distinct group of middle-class and upper-middle-class single men and women—mostly women—who are adopting children from foster care, from orphanages in other countries, and through adoption agencies and attorneys in the United States. Most are *very* happy that they adopted.

Many of the issues surrounding adoption are the same for both single and married people: What is it like to be a parent? Am I ready to be a parent? Could I bond to an adopted child? and so forth. But the single person who is trying to decide for or against adoption faces some unique issues. Those issues are the focus of this chapter.

IS FERTILITY A FACTOR
FOR SINGLE ADOPTIVE PARENTS?

Some single men and women who have been married before have sought to have a biological child with their spouse, but discovered a fertility problem. Some single women who have never been married decide to bear a biological child, but then learn that they are infertile. Others have never sought a pregnancy and have probably always used birth control. These women do not really know if they could achieve a pregnancy, but many believe it is better to adopt a child who is "already here."

There are many reasons why some single women do not seek a pregnancy. Perhaps they don't have a personal tie to a man they wish to become impregnated by. Or perhaps they don't like the anonymity of a donor insemination, either because the idea of it feels uncomfortable to them or because they have moral or religious concerns about it. They may not wish to have a biological child because of genetic problems in their own background that they don't wish to pass on.

Men have many of the same reasons as do women for not seeking a pregnancy, but they can also have specific reasons. For example, a single man may not wish to impregnate a woman he knows because he may fear that she could leave him and take the child away.

Carol is a single mom who adopted her child from an orphanage in India. Carol believes (and is probably right) that if she had not adopted her daughter, the child would have continued to live in miserable circumstances.

CONSIDERING YOUR LIFESTYLE

Singles don't always have a backup person. (And yes, married people do divorce, so married people can become single people.) As a result, *all* the parenting tasks, from getting the child up in the morning to making sure the child is safe in bed at night, fall on the single person. This can be daunting for even the most competent parent. It is still true today that most wives shoulder the brunt of child care. But at the least, married women have someone they can fall back on for help—the husband.

As a result, singles who are considering adoption need to take a very hard look at what sort of support system they have in their lives and at whom they could ask for help in a pinch. For example, if you became too ill to care for the child, who could watch him or her? If you needed to go on a business trip, whom could you rely upon to either house-sit or take care of your child in their home?

It's essential that you decide these issues ahead of time. Do not wait for a minor or major crisis to occur and then panic at solving the problem. Believe it or not, some people do this.

DEALING WITH ADOPTION AGENCIES
AND ATTORNEYS

Agencies may often seek to push single people into adopting children with special needs—for example, older children or children with medical or emotional problems. In many cases, these children need more attention than does the average adopted child. It may be very hard for a single person to parent a child who has special needs. However, some people believe that singles are in a unique position to parent a child who has been damaged by life—because the single person is not "distracted" by the needs of a significant other, he or she can devote a great deal of attention to the child. In addition, the single person might eventually marry.

There are many adoption agencies that will accept single people. This does not mean that every single person who applies to adopt will be welcomed with open arms. Applicants must go through the same home study process as all other prospective adoptive parents.

Adoption attorneys vary on their own opinions of single adoptive parenthood; some are opposed, others are not. The single person should be able to quickly discover what the lawyer's bias is after talking to him or her.

MAKING THE DECISION

Hope Marindin, director of the National Council for Single Adoptive Parents in Chevy Chase, Maryland, believes that single people have two primary issues to consider when contemplating an adoption: First, analyze the depth of your desire to have a child. Marindin thinks that the intensity of your desire to adopt outweighs all other factors. She says that whether you have managed a Girl Scout troop in the past, taught religious classes to children, and so forth is irrelevant, and that the only significant factor is how strong your personal desire is to adopt. It's up to you to decide the intensity of your desire. I believe that past activities with children may sometimes be an indicator of your potential interest as a parent. But it is certainly not the only indicator. I agree with Marindin that the urge to adopt is paramount.

Second, says Marindin, is determining how you will afford the fees of adoption. She believes that most singles can afford to adopt.

If you are not sure about whether you should adopt, it might help to attend adoptive parent group meetings and meet parents and their children. Some singles enjoy the support they receive from a group that embraces both couples and singles, whereas others prefer to attend a singles-only support group when one is available.

Reading helps. The more you learn about adoption and adopted kids, the better prepared you will be to make your decision. Read general parenting books, too. Do they intrigue you just a little bit? Are you eager to learn more? (Not all parenting books are well written, so if you are left cold after reading one, that does not mean you would make a bad parent.)

WHAT DO YOUR PARENTS AND FRIENDS THINK?

Take into account what kind of psychological support you can expect from parents and peers. One study on single adoptive parents found distinctive differences when parents approved of the adoption.

In a group who stated that their parents thought adoption was a good idea and were very approving, 80 percent believed their children had shown an excellent adjustment to the adoption. Conversely, when parents were negative, indifferent, or had mixed reactions, only 40 percent believed their children had adjusted well. Thus, there was a clear indicator that family support played a strong role in the success of an adoption.

If you are a single person who is seriously considering adoption or if you've already decided you want to adopt a child, check with adoptive parent groups nationwide. They usually know of agencies that specifically do accept single applicants. Check Appendix B for parent groups, and also check other resources such as *Report on Intercountry Adoption*, published by International Concerns for Children in Boulder, Colorado. Also be sure to read Hope Marindin's publication, *The Handbook for Single Adoptive Parents* (available for $20 from the National Council for Single Adoptive Parents, P.O. Box 15084, Chevy Chase, MD 20825).

PART THREE

LOOKING OUTWARD— QUESTIONS TO ASK OTHERS

9

TALKING TO FAMILY
AND FRIENDS
ABOUT ADOPTION

If you have not decided yet whether you should adopt, should you keep it to yourself that you are considering adoption or should you share it with others? There are advantages and disadvantages to each approach, and this chapter covers both sides of the question.

ADVANTAGES OF TELLING
YOUR FAMILY

One advantage of telling your family that you are thinking about adopting a child is that you can get a lot of emotional baggage out of the way. "My feeling is I would tell them you're thinking about it," says attorney Vika Andrel of Andrel Adoptions in Austin, Texas. "You're going to have to deal with their attitudes and you need to know, is your mother going to be able to accept this child as her real honest-to-God grandchild or is she going to treat her differently from her other grandchildren? You need to know about this beforehand. And if you can't figure out how you're going to deal with it, maybe you should rethink whether adoption is the right thing for you."

Another advantage is that the family will have a chance to get used to the idea of having a family member who is adopted. "The family needs time to prepare, too," says Mary Beth Style, M.S.W., and former vice president of professional practice for the National Council For Adoption in Washington, D.C. "I don't think it's fair to announce 'We're going to the adoption agency to pick up the baby now,' if that's the first your family has heard about you being interested in adoption."

PROBLEMS WITH TELLING YOUR FAMILY

One problem with telling your family you are investigating adoption or that you plan to adopt is that you may be overwhelmed with constant inquiries of "Did you get a baby yet?" to a maddening level. Here's a trick that can work. Tell your family that it'll take four or five years to adopt, and then they won't bother you about it. When you adopt in a year or so, they will be pleasantly surprised.

If you do talk to your family about adoption, don't be shocked if you receive plenty of negative feedback—it goes with the territory. There are far too many people who will be eager to tell you to adopt or not adopt, but it is a decision that you should make yourself after an informed look at yourself and at adoption and adopted children in general.

TELLING YOUR FRIENDS

If you choose to confide to your friends that you are thinking about adopting a child, expect to receive the same possible range of reactions as you might get from your family. Some friends will be very supportive, whereas others may be very dubious. Still others may try to talk you out of adoption altogether—or they may try to talk you *into* adoption before you feel ready.

Some friends will have heard of someone with a bad experience, or they may have a negative opinion about adoption for some reason. Some may be simply baffled by the topic altogether.

Good friends will listen to you and try to help you if they can. But do understand that even good friends have their own biases and prejudices, both pro and con. You may find that your friends begin clipping articles from magazines and newspapers about adoption. If they are informative pieces, you will probably appreciate the information; if they are all horror stories, you probably will not.

COPING WITH PROBING QUESTIONS

Once your family and friends know that you are considering adoption, it's almost inevitable that you will be the recipient of some very intrusive questions and a certain amount of unwanted advice. The subjects of infertility and adoption seem to be topics that everybody has an opinion on and is eager to share with you. If you find that people are asking you probing questions, remember that you do not have to answer them.

Even if you feel your spouse is very comfortable about people knowing there is a problem with infertility, don't be so sure that you're right. For example, a man may not want the world to know that his sperm count is low, and a woman may not want everyone (especially that gossipy Cousin Sue) to know that she has damaged fallopian tubes.

These are private matters and it's pretty likely that neither person will wish to have them debated endlessly over the dinner table at Thanksgiving. Another problem is that others may speculate that the infertility problem is someone's "fault," when assigning blame is the last thing you need to deal with.

If the probing questions are about adoption, such as How can you afford to adopt a child? and Why in the world do you really want to adopt? you can close the door to the subject if you want to. Ask them *why* they want to know, or simply tell them that it's a private matter. And don't explain.

EDUCATE YOURSELF FIRST

My best advice is to learn as much as you can about adoption. Read pertinent books, and talk with social workers, attorneys, and adoptive parent groups. When you are educated about adoption, you can better counter the myths, fears, and concerns that people in your family may have with adoption. After all, what they know about adoption may be limited to a highlight on the evening news that focused on a Movie of the Week about some adoption disaster. They don't realize that thousands of adoptions go through each year without a hitch.

You will also be able to answer questions such as "Why don't you just go to an orphanage and pick out your baby?" Some people still think you can do that. (Of course, you can't do that in the United States, and only rarely can you do it in other countries.)

TAKE INTO ACCOUNT
YOUR FAMILY SITUATION

How close—both physically and emotionally—are you to your family? AnnaMarie Merrill, editor of *Report on Intercountry Adoption* (an excellent resource for international adopters), says if your parents live next door to you and would play a large part in your child's life, then it may be a good idea to involve them in your adoption plan earlier than you would if they lived a thousand miles away.

Even if your family lives far away, how emotionally close are you to them? If your parents or siblings would disapprove of adoption, would this stop you from applying? It's better to find this out *before* you adopt your child.

IT'S REALLY UP TO YOU

It should be clear to you by now that whether you tell your family should be your own decision, one made only after carefully weighing the pros and cons and your own feelings about sharing the information. You may be surprised to find that your family is very supportive and helpful.

I have talked to people who wanted to become grandparents, and when they learned their son or daughter was interested in adoption, they dropped everything to call agencies, buy books, and educate themselves as much as possible. Sometimes they also attend adoptive parent group meetings.

As a former leader of an adoptive parent group, I can tell you that we had visitors who wanted to become grandparents, aunts, uncles, and even siblings to an adopted child. One prospective parent brought her seventeen-year-old daughter to meetings, and they both asked numerous questions and even took notes. (And yes, the family did ultimately adopt three older children.)

On the other hand, I have known people who assumed that their parents would be very supportive. Instead, they were shocked that their relatives were very disapproving. It's personal when it comes to your family.

Weigh all the factors and decide what is right for you. I have summarized the pros and cons of telling your family in the chart below.

Pros and Cons of Telling Your Family You're Considering Adoption

Pros	Cons
The family will have time to become used to the idea.	They may ask too many probing questions.
You'll know if they are accepting.	They may try to talk you out of adopting.
They can provide assistance.	They may want details about your infertility that you don't want to share.
They may empathize.	They may want to tell you about their own problems with infertility or other issues.
	They may joke and ask you if you want their children.
They can help you gather information.	They may tell you stories of adoptions that went wrong, adopted people who had severe problems, etc.
They can offer to babysit for you after you adopt, if needed.	They may reject the idea of adoption.
They may see adoption as helping a child and as being a very positive goal.	They may see adoption as taking on "someone else's problems."
They may build you up when you are discouraged.	They may tell you that feeling down is a "sign" that you should not do this.

10

WILL COUNSELING HELP WITH YOUR DECISION?

If you feel you have expended considerable time thinking about adoption and discussing all the pros and cons with your spouse and yet you're still "not there yet," you may want to seek a psychologist or therapist to help you work out the key issues. Some individuals specialize in "preadoption counseling," or "infertility/adoption counseling." A good counselor can help you to identify the issues and how you feel about them as well as suggest ways to help you move toward a decision.

You do not have to be mentally ill to see a psychologist or therapist. Many normal people consult with therapists to help them resolve difficult issues.

COUNSELING IS NOT ALWAYS NECESSARY

Of course, not every serious life decision requires counseling. You or you and your spouse often make difficult decisions without having to consult with a therapist. You may be able to resolve problems by discussing them with your spouse or among friends or by attending support group meetings or by reading books. Religious people find that prayer and meditation can be very helpful in leading them toward the decision that is right for them.

Your health insurance may not cover counseling fees, or maybe you do not want your health insurance company to know that you have sought counseling and you would rather pay the fees yourself. (Fees can run from about $75 an hour and up, depending on the type of therapy, the therapist, and so forth.)

PROACTIVE, REACTIVE, OR ACQUIESCENT: WHICH ARE YOU?

C. Michael Snyter, a clinical psychologist (and an adoptive parent) in Glenside, Pennsylvania, counsels individuals who are thinking about adoption. He says he begins with finding out why they want children. In addition, says Snyter, "I try to discern if they are approaching adoption as a proactive person, a reactive person, or an acquiescent person."

A proactive person is someone who has learned about adoption, feels good about it, and has a healthy perspective. The reactive person is on the rebound, angry, and actively grieving. "They don't care, give me a kid today is their attitude and that's not healthy," says Snyter. An acquiescent person has the attitude, "I can't have a child, I guess there's no choice, I have to adopt,"—also an unhealthy attitude. Snyter works to move people toward proactive decisions, whether they choose to adopt or not.

In addition, he feels it's important to consider a "childfree" life, because he believes that adoption cannot truly be chosen unless other alternatives are considered and then rejected.

Snyter says that another key factor is *not* to rush your decision. Don't give yourself a deadline to decide, like next week or next month. Instead, learn as much as possible about adoption and consider your choices.

FINDING A GOOD THERAPIST

If you do decide to seek counseling, finding the right therapist depends on what you want resolved. Are you seeking one who is knowledgeable about the problems related to decision making about infertility and/or adoption? In that case, you can seek recommendations from the nearest infertility support group, such as the local RESOLVE chapter.

You may also believe that a good general therapist should be able to assist most people who are trying to work through a major life-changing decision. Your medical doctor may be able to recommend psychologists, psychiatrists, and therapists in your area.

If you do ask support groups for recommendations of therapists in the area, you do not have to raise your hand at a meeting and publicly ask for the information. You should be able to call a leader or another person in the organization to obtain this information privately.

Consider whether you would be more comfortable with individual counseling or with group therapy. (Some people will use both options.) If you feel you would be comfortable with sharing information with people who have a similar problem, then you may find group therapy to be effective. It may also be less expensive. (Check first, however. Do not assume that group therapy is invariably less costly.)

Of course, group therapy does not work for everyone. Some people are very private and cannot discuss problems in a group setting; thus, they prefer individual therapy sessions. Be sure that the therapist can provide the type of therapy, group or private, that you want.

Beware of anti-adoption groups that masquerade as "adoption support groups." These people actually believe that adoption is very bad. Ask them for past issues of newsletters and read them. Attend one or two meetings. If only negative issues and problems are discussed, this is a bad sign. One group passes out tissues at the beginning of their adoption seminars! This is a sign that they see adoption in a very negative light, because they assume you are inevitably going to cry.

Of course, adoption is not a perfect institution, and problems exist. But a group that focuses on the problems of adoption and very rarely talks about the rewards, is not a group that will help you.

Adoption Orientation

When seeking a counselor, find out if the therapist has any hidden agendas. Ask them if they have any ties to adoption—either as an adoptive parent, adopted person, or birthparent. It does not mean that you should not consult with them if they do have these ties. As mentioned earlier, such ties can be extremely beneficial in providing you with the help and information you need. But it is important to know about them beforehand so you can be aware of any possible biases, pro or con, that the therapist may have about adoption.

Types of Counselors

There are many types of mental health professionals. The most highly educated are psychiatrists—physicians who specialize in psychiatry. Psychiatrists frequently treat "normal" people, and you do not have to be mentally ill to see a psychiatrist; however, psychiatric fees can be expensive, and many psychiatrists may be unable to give you the type of counseling that you need. They can prescribe medications, including antidepressants.

Psychologists are individuals with a Ph.D. in psychology or counseling. A good psychologist can often help you sort out your major issues and offer you advice on how to resolve them. They are not allowed to prescribe medication.

Therapists and social workers also provide counseling to people with problems of infertility who are considering adoption. A therapist may have a master's degree in psychology or counseling; a social worker usually has a master's in social work.

ASK QUESTIONS FIRST

Many therapists are willing to talk to you briefly on the phone for no fee before you sign up for your first visit. When you feel you have found one who might be a good counselor for you, ask the secretary if it would be possible for you to have such a short discussion beforehand. Be sure to explain that you are not seeking free advice but rather trying to decide if this counselor would be the one to help you with your problem. And don't take advantage of the counselor—certainly in ten or fifteen minutes at most you should obtain the information you need.

As you talk to the counselor, see if this person sounds like someone you could talk to, someone who is professional and at the same time can be empathetic and understanding.

Here is a brief list of questions you may wish to ask. Also, be sure to add your own questions to this list or change these questions to suit your needs.

1.   Have you ever helped a person who is trying to decide whether to adopt a child?
2.   How do you feel about adoption? (The person who is very negative about adoption or euphorically positive is probably the wrong counselor for you. You need someone who is willing to be neutral so that you will not feel pressed toward or away from adoption.)
3.   Do you rely primarily on group or individual therapy for this type of issue? (Define the issue for the therapist: You want assistance with deciding whether you should adopt a child.)

4. How many sessions do you think it might take to help resolve this issue? Most counselors will equivocate on this question because they do not want to tell you it will take exactly eight or ten sessions—in case a few more are indicated. Tell the therapist you want a "ballpark" idea, a range. Rarely should you need extensive counseling for six months or longer for an issue like this. If the therapist says you do need more than six months to resolve the issue—up front, without even seeing you first—find another therapist.

5. Do you have any personal knowledge of adoption, as either an adoptive parent, an adopted person, or a birthparent? Or in any other role? (The counselor may have worked for an adoption agency, although this is unlikely. Ask anyway. He or she may have counseled adopted children and could have developed biases.)

GROUP SESSIONS
AREN'T NECESSARILY GLOOMY
AND DOOMY

Dr. Snyter says that people are surprised to learn that many of his preadoptive sessions are full of laughter and are very upbeat. "People feel good because they're in a room where they feel safe. All the other people are in the same boat, and they can relate to them and let their defenses down. It's a very positive experience."

It's also a confidential experience as well, and Snyter does not provide information to anyone outside the group or even acknowledge that he has particular couples in his group. His groups of ten or twelve people meet once a week for about ten weeks and they are comprised of the same people who started at the beginning. He does not like bringing in new people during the ten-week period because it would disrupt the flow of the group.

COUNSELING
FOR SECONDARY INFERTILITY

Dr. Snyter offers separate groups for individuals with secondary infertility, because often people with primary infertility cannot empathize with someone who already has one or more children and cannot have more. Snyter says, "The reality is that secondary infertility is emotionally more difficult for two reasons. One, you get even less understanding and empathy from people, who say, 'You've got a child, don't be greedy.' Another reason is that you've had an opportunity to sample what parenting is all about and now that you've had it, you want it even more."

COUNSELING CAN BE EFFECTIVE

When you are stymied and perplexed by the difficult decision about whether you should adopt a child, you may find that a good counselor can help you work through the decision-making morass and come to a conclusion. Many people do not need counseling to make their choice, but others find that counseling gives them the extra help they need.

Be sure to screen the counselor and whenever possible, ask the counselor key questions before your first session. If this is not possible, ask them during the first session. If you are unhappy with the answers, then find another counselor.

Some counselors may tell you that you have other issues to resolve, such as problems with your own parents or with your marriage or something else. If you agree, then this counselor may be able to aid you in working through these issues. If you don't agree, you may be right and the counselor could be reading you wrong—in that case, find another counselor.

11

GATHERING
INFORMATION

Your friends and family may not really understand what you are going through when you are trying to decide whether to adopt—even if you explain it to them as plainly as you can. But there are other people who usually do understand, people who are going through pretty much the same thing as you, or who have already gone through it—and many are eager to help.

RESOLVE MAY BE ABLE TO HELP

RESOLVE is a national support group for individuals who are seeking to become parents, either biologically or through adoption. RESOLVE has chapters throughout the country and can provide you with a great deal of information on the various fertility options as well as the many psychological ramifications of this struggle you face.

RESOLVE can also provide some adoption information and point you to adoptive parent groups in your area. You can contact their national office at 1310 Broadway, Somerville, Massachusetts 02144-1731, or call the helpline phone number, 617-623-0744. (Also see listings of state RESOLVE offices in Appendix B.)

If you think that you may need some professional help, perhaps a therapist to assist you in sorting out all the issues, your local RESOLVE should be able to recommend someone.

ADOPTIVE PARENTS GROUPS MAY HELP

If you feel that you are leaning more toward adoption, you may wish to contact local adoptive parent groups right away for more information. You do not have to reveal your life story at group meetings. You can merely say that you are there to listen and learn, and members should be willing to respect this.

Do realize, however, that adoptive parents are prone to expound on the joys of adoption and sometimes may subtly pressure you to contact agencies or attorneys before you feel ready. Their intent is good, but you must stand firm. Don't proceed with adoption unless and until the time feels right to you.

See Appendix B for listings of adoptive parent support groups; however, do keep in mind that such groups change leadership frequently because of the volunteer nature of the organization. In most cases, when one leader steps down, a new leader or even a new group steps in to fill the gap.

A Broad Variety of Groups Exists

There are hundreds of adoptive parent support groups nationwide. Some are umbrellaed under large organizations; many are small groups of as few as twenty people who get together informally to share information. Some adoptive parent groups concentrate on adoption in the United States, primarily because their members have adopted or wish to adopt children in this country. Other groups center on international adoption for the same reason—members have adopted or wish to adopt children from other countries.

The Group's Orientation and Attitude Does Matter

It's easy to see that the orientation of the group affects its attitude; thus, the international adoption group may have very negative feelings about adopting a child through an attorney or agency in the United States, whereas the U.S. adoption group may be fearful of problems that kids from other countries might have.

You can sometimes tell the orientation of a group from its name. For example, if the group name includes the name of a foreign country, then you can presume their members' main interests lie in adoptions from that country.

You can learn a lot about adoption and adoptive parents (and their children) by attending meetings of adoptive parent groups. You can observe these parents interacting with their children and with each other. In addition, you can gain a feel for what their problems are and how they are like and unlike the problems of most parents.

Finding a Group

Here are some tips on how to make the best use of an adoptive parent group:

- Find at least two or three adoptive parent groups within a hundred-mile radius of your home, and attend at least one meeting of each group. Although you probably won't be able to attend every meeting of the faraway group, it may be the one group with the information you need.
- Don't attend a planning meeting or a party first. These are atypical and don't give you a feel for the group. Ask the group's leader if the meeting will be a typical meeting and seek to attend one of them. Later, try attending a picnic or party that the group is having.
- Find out if the group has invited any adoption agency social workers or attorneys to speak at its meeting. Will the speaker dominate the whole meeting? You need a chance to ask questions comfortably, so find out if the speaker will remain at the entire meeting. On the other hand, if you have already decided that you want to adopt, use this informal setting and relaxed atmosphere to learn about the policies and practices of the agency or attorney.

ONLINE GROUPS AND WEB SITES

With the availability of the Internet as well as other online services, some people may think they can use their computers to collect most of the information they need to successfully adopt. But the problem with online information, especially that found on the Internet, is that it may be solely based on personal opinions. This is particularly true of information given out on "newsgroups" or web sites.

Excited new adoptive parents who want to share their information with the world often create their own web site. Unfortunately, the only expertise they usually have is limited to their own personal experience.

A Proliferation of Adoption Web Sites

In early 1997, I did a search on the Internet using the word "adoption" and found 4,063 sites! Of course, some of these were for "adopting" dogs, ferrets, and other animals, but many were for the adoption of children. There is a lot of information out there to wade through!

Some very helpful sites have been created by state government agencies or by excellent adoption agencies. But problem sites exist as well. As a result, it can be very difficult, even for a person who is knowledgeable about adoption and about the Internet, to separate what is valid and what is not true at all.

Drawbacks to Advertising Yourself on the Internet

Some people are actually advertising their desire to adopt on the Internet, using it as a sort of high-tech classified ad service. Attorney Douglas Donnelly of Santa Barbara, California, who wrote the code of ethics for the American Academy of Adoption Attorneys, sees this as a risky proposition. Although he does not have any clients who have advertised on the Internet, he has known people who have advertised in the classified sections of newspapers.

Donnelly says, "I recommend against advertising, period. I think it leaves you very vulnerable. Every person I know who has advertised in the personals columns has received a collect call, usually at two in the morning, from someone saying, 'I'm six months pregnant and worried sick about what to do about my baby and you're the answer to my prayers! Oh, and by the way, I'm being evicted from my apartment tomorrow morning for not paying the rent. Could you wire me $500 before ten o'clock?' "

The probability that the gullible prospective parent will actually adopt this woman's child (if she is even pregnant) is very close to zero. Donnelly says it's far better to rely on personal contacts and networking in locating a birthmother. If there are no groups nearby, you can always check out CompuServe, America Online, or the Internet for adoption information. But, as mentioned earlier, take the advice offered on online services with a very generous dose of salt—people often have many biases and hidden agendas, and thus you need to maintain a critical detachment.

Some state social services offices, such as those in New York and Florida, provide information on adopting children in foster care. There are also many adoptive parent groups who post information about their organization on a web site.

Both the Internet and America Online's Adoption Forum are wonderful opportunities for quick information gathering for today's future adoptive parents. Be careful, have fun, and maybe you will find the information you need or even a photo that will lead you to your child. (See Appendix B for a listing of selected Internet adoption sites.)

OTHER RESOURCES

There are a variety of information sources other than adoptive parent groups or what you can find on the Internet. For example, many agencies that are still not on the Internet can provide informational brochures on their organizations. Also, if you would like to learn more about available adoption materials for sale, why not ask your local parent group? Many subscribe to publications and may display them at their monthly meetings. This offers you an opportunity to preview material before you buy.

Organizational Resources

Some organizations, such as Los Niños in The Woodlands, Texas, or Adoptions From the Heart in Ardmore, Pennsylvania, create excellent informational newsletters. Many attorneys offer brochures on their services—be sure to ask. Some organizations also lend or sell videotapes.

The National Council For Adoption in Washington, D.C., offers free information on how to find agencies and attorneys in their hotline adoption packet. Call them at 202-328-1200 or write to them at 1930 Seventeenth St., N.W., Washington, DC 20009.

Adoptive Families of America (AFA) in St. Paul, Minnesota, offers "A Guide to Adoption" for prospective parents. Send $4.95 (includes postage and handling) to AFA, 2309 Como Ave., St. Paul, MN 55108. If you have a question or a problem with a particular agency, call AFA at 1-800-372-3300.

Books, Magazines, and Newsletters

An array of books on adoption is available. Many focus on explaining adoption to children or on how to parent adopted children. Some are how-to books on adopting an infant and/or an older child; some explain about open adoption. Psychologists and therapists have written on many different adoption topics. Many of these books may not be available on the shelves in your local bookstore, but you should ask if you can order them. A large bookstore can order most that are still in print. You could also ask the reference librarian at your local library to help you in finding a book and then in ordering it for you through Interlibrary Loan.

Author and publisher Patricia Johnston has written and/or published good titles on adoption. Contact her at Perspectives Press, P.O. Box 90318, Indianapolis, IN 46290. (Her web site is http://www.PerspectivesPress.com.) Her most recent title, *Launching a Baby's Adoption: Practical Strategies for Parents and Professionals*, is a helpful book with plenty of good advice for new adoptive parents of infants.

Virtually all adoption books are also available through Tapestry Books. Ask for their free catalog by calling them at 1-800-765-2367.

The most prominent adoption magazine is *Adoptive Families*, published every other month by Adoptive Families of America ($24.95 per year). Another interesting magazine is *ROOTS & WINGS*, published quarterly by ROOTS & WINGS Publications (P.O. Box 577, Hackettstown, NJ 07840) for $19.95 per year.

Far too many newsletters on adoption are published to list them all. But I think the newsletter published by the Adoptive Parents Committee (APC) in New York is very informative and useful—even if you don't live in New York. Contact APC at P.O. Box 3525, Church St. Station, New York, NY 10008-3525.

Adoption/Medical News is a newsletter that describes a variety of medical conditions and medical problems. It's primarily of interest to adoption professionals and parent groups, but it has many individual subscribers as well. This publication is produced ten times per year for $36 (Adoption Advocates Press, 1921 Ohio St. NE, Palm Bay, FL 32907).

Author Lois Melina produces *Adopted Child*, a monthly newsletter that concentrates on one topic per month and covers many intriguing issues related to adoption. The publication is $22 (Adopted Child, P.O. Box 9362, Moscow, ID 83843).

If you are interested in the adoption of older children and other children with special needs, *Adoptalk* is a good quarterly publication produced by the North American Council on Adoptable Children (NACAC). Individual membership (which includes the newsletter) is $40. Contact them at 970 Raymond Ave., Ste. 106, St. Paul, MN 55114-1149.

If you are interested in the latest news and issues on adoption, *National Adoption Reports*, published by the National Council For Adoption, is a good monthly source. Write to them at NCFA, 1930 Seventeenth St. N.W., Washington, DC 20009, or call 202-328-1200.

PART FOUR

ADOPTION ISSUES AND INFORMATION

12

ADOPTING
FROM THE UNITED STATES

Yes, it is possible to adopt a child from the United States, whether you wish to adopt an infant or older child, a healthy white infant or a biracial child, or a child with special needs. This chapter concentrates not on the "hows" but rather on the types of adoption in the United States.

There are many myths associated with adopting children from the United States (see Chapter 1). This chapter is a short one because much relevant information is included in other chapters, such as the ones on open adoption, transracial adoption, and adopting children with special needs. Also, be sure to read Chapter 18, which includes information on medical issues for adopted children.

ADOPTING
THROUGH STATE AGENCIES

There are two types of adoption agencies: (1) public agencies managed by the state or county, and (2) private agencies. State or county agencies concentrate on placing foster children for adoption—in general, children who have been removed from their parents because of abuse, neglect, or abandonment.

Foster parents care for the child until he or she is returned to the parent or until the state decides to involuntarily take away ("terminate") the parental rights of the biological parents. This is a very difficult process and it usually takes years before termination occurs.

You can become a foster parent and care for a child for years, and if the child becomes "free" for adoption, you are often the first family considered. In some cases, however, foster parents are not considered to adopt the child. Check with social workers in your state or county to find out the policy in your area. Or you could choose not to be a foster parent and instead enter the system as an adoptive parent applicant only. In this case, you will adopt a child who has been in foster care, often for a minimum of three or four years and usually a lot longer. Obviously, in most cases, the child who is placed for adoption will be at least six or seven.

PRIVATE ADOPTION AGENCIES

Private agencies are licensed by the state to place children. They are generally nonprofit organizations and are often run by people who have degrees in social work or psychology.

Some agencies have a specific orientation; for example, they may seek applicants who are members of a particular religious group and who profess certain views supported by the agency. Others see themselves as a sort of professional intermediary between birthparents and adoptive parents, and they believe that the "choosing" should be done by the parties themselves, with some help.

Some agencies place only U.S. children. Others specialize in international adoption, but some international adoption agencies handle a few U.S. adoptions as well.

ATTORNEYS
AND INDEPENDENT ADOPTION

Independent adoption refers to non-agency adoption. In some states, attorneys may handle all the details of locating birthmothers and matching them to adoptive parents; whereas in other states, the "job" of finding a birthmother is left to the adoptive parents. The attorney concentrates on making sure that the legalities are followed.

Sometimes "adoption facilitators" assist families in locating birthparents. Whether someone other than a social worker or an attorney may legally assume this role depends on the state that you live in. Some states, such as Florida, forbid anyone but attorneys and adoption agencies from receiving payment for making adoption referrals.

RESOURCES

There are many issues involved in agency adoption, and a good how-to book on adoption can help you understand the primary points as well as the nuances of adopting a child from the United States. *There ARE Babies to Adopt: A Resource Guide for Prospective Parents*, updated in 1996, offers guidance. *The Legal Adoption Guide: Safely Navigating the System* by Colleen Alexander-Roberts offers assistance on adopting independently in the United States.

13

MYTHS AND REALITIES OF INTERNATIONAL ADOPTION

International adoption is subject to many myths, but the reality is that over 11,000 children were adopted from other countries in 1996, up from 9,700 in 1995. About 3,700 of the children were adopted from Europe, and about 3,400 were adopted from China. Korean adoptions, which used to be in the majority, have fallen from a high of over 6,000 in 1986 to about 1,500 in 1996.

Currently, children are being adopted from many countries, including Bolivia, Brazil, China, Columbia, Costa Rica, Ecuador, Guatemala, India, Korea, Mexico, Nepal, Paraguay, the Philippines, Romania, Russian Republic, Thailand, Ukraine, Vietnam, and others.

MAJOR MYTHS ABOUT INTERNATIONAL ADOPTION

Myth #1: It's Easy to Adopt from Another Country.

Actually, the ease of adoption depends on the country. It also depends on the timing, who is in power in the government, and many other factors. Currently, many people are adopting children from China. Several years ago, there were virtually no adoptions from China. A country can "open" or "close" its doors to adoption at any time and for any reason.

Myth #2: Children from Orphanages
Are Heartier Because They've Survived.

Many people believe that if a child does not die in a foreign orphanage, then the child must be basically healthy. Children who do not die in orphanages may or may not have and continue to have serious health problems. Adopting parents should gain as much information as possible about any child they plan to adopt.

Some adopters mistakenly believe that a foreign child who is developmentally delayed is somehow different from a U.S. child who is developmentally delayed. As a result, some people adopt children from foreign orphanages who have problems that the adoptive parents would never consider accepting in a child from the United States.

Children are children, the world over. And problems are problems, the world over. For example, if a child from Brazil truly has a developmental delay, Fetal Alcohol Syndrome, or some other problem, adopting parents will face the same issues that they would face had they adopted a child born in the United States with these problems.

Myth #3: Children from Orphanages
Are Never Abused.

For some reason, the myth persists that children living in orphanages overseas were never physically abused, unlike their counterparts in U.S. foster care. The truth is that many older children from orphanages around the world have faced abuse from many sources.

Myth #4: All Foreign-Born Children
Come from Terrible Backgrounds
and No Healthy Babies Are Available.

As already mentioned, orphanages vary greatly, not only from country to country but also within countries. Some children from other countries come from backgrounds of serious neglect and others are basically healthy. Foreign-born infants may have some medical problems or they may be healthy.

Myth #5: Foreign Birthmothers
Never Change Their Minds

This myth is close to reality. Birthmothers from other countries rarely change their minds about adoption, and usually the agency or orphanage has custody of the child. But "never say never." There *are* cases where foreign birthmothers have sought to regain their children and have succeeded.

Some people are fearful of adopting a child from the United States, primarily because of the fear of the birthparents changing their minds about adoption. Consequently, these people choose international adoption—or no adoption.

Myth #6: A Good Home Can Erase
All Previous Problems

This is a variation of the "love conquers all" myth. Medical or emotional problems that children have will not evaporate just because you are nice to them or because you love them. If you decide to adopt a child who has problems, then you need to be willing to help the child with those problems. Many children adopted from other countries have flourished under the care their adoptive parents provided.

Myth #7: (Believed by Some Foreign Citizens):
Adopters Have Evil Motives.

One of the saddest myths about international adoption was perpetrated over a decade ago by the former Soviet Union, when its relations with the United States were at best unfriendly. Disinformation campaigns reported that Americans were adopting children from other countries for nefarious purposes: to use them to stuff their bodies with cocaine and thus transport illegal drugs; to use their body parts for transplants; to use them as slaves.

Even though the disinformation ended long ago, such rumors spring up periodically. For example, several years ago an Alaskan woman was disabled for life when she visited Guatemala on business. A mob believed that she was there to take "their" children and to accomplish evil deeds upon them, and they severely attacked her. In fact, she was not interested in adoption at all. Such situations are extremely rare, but it's important to realize that when you visit another land, it is *you* who are the outsider.

REALITIES
OF INTERNATIONAL ADOPTION

Reality #1: Federal Requirements Are Important

One unifying element in international adoption is the U.S. Immigration and Naturalization Service (INS). This government agency oversees international adoption, and anyone from the United States who wants to adopt a child from another country must comply with its requirements. (This does not mean, however, that if something goes wrong, the INS will solve the problem for you.)

For example, prospective adopter(s) must first obtain an approved home study before they may adopt. A few states do not require a home study, but the federal requirements supersede the state ones, unless the state requirements are stricter than the federal ones.

The INS also requires that the child must receive a physical examination before entering the United States, and she or he will receive a special visa based on the parents' American passports. If the U.S. Embassy–approved doctor identifies certain serious medical problems (too many to name here), the adopters must sign a waiver that states they know about the child's disability and will take responsibility for the child. However, passing this physical is *no guarantee* of good health. Visa medical examinations vary greatly from country to country.

At least one parent in an adopting couple must be a U.S. citizen to adopt a child into the United States. The child will later be "naturalized," or become a U.S. citizen based on the parents' citizenship; however, the adoptive parents must apply for this citizenship—it is not automatically done by some government employee.

This makes the process sound simple, but there are countless papers and forms to sign. If the language spoken in the child's country of origin is not English, then in most cases, you must provide that country's officials with translations of all English documents.

Reality #2: Orphanage Conditions Vary Greatly

Orphanage conditions can vary greatly even within a country, with some orphanages being well managed and others having atrocious conditions. Many people still remember the television news coverage of the terrible conditions at some Romanian orphanages in the early 1990s. Those scenes inspired thousands of people, including some who were very ill-prepared, to adopt children from Romania.

Reality #3: Health Problems of Children from Other Countries Vary

Health problems that the foreign child may have can be very different from or very similar to the health problems of a child adopted from the United States. For example, the child could have tuberculosis or hepatitis B or even be HIV positive. The child could also test positive for syphilis, and even though a foreign doctor may say the child was treated, treatment could have been one brief injection that was insufficient to kill the germs.

Although the American Academy of Pediatrics has standard screening tests for children adopted from other countries, most U.S. pediatricians are not trained in what to look for. A child's stool should be examined for parasites, and a hepatitis B profile should be done.

Other tests are also needed. The doctor should be able to obtain the necessary information through the American Academy of Pediatrics or by contacting the International Adoption Clinic at the University of Minnesota in Minneapolis.

If you are planning to adopt a child from a foreign country, you should also make sure that you find a pediatrician *before* your child arrives. If the doctor you choose does not know much about caring for internationally adopted children, it's important that he or she be willing to learn. You do not need the hassle of having to search for a good doctor after your child arrives.

A child who is diagnosed with a disorder in another country may be diagnosed differently in the United States. Conversely, a child who is deemed healthy by officials in another country may be viewed as having a health or emotional problem in the United States. Of course, doctors should make allowances for the radical acculturation that newly arrived children have to make and for the difficult behavior that may result. Only very extreme and endangering behavior may need a rapid evaluation, and the doctor should always be advised that the child is new to the country.

Reality #4: International Adoption Usually Means Racial and Cultural Differences

A child from another country may be of a different race from you. And even if the child is of your race, he or she will certainly come from a different culture. An older child will be used to ways that are very different from your own.

Some adoptive parents take great pains to expose their child to cultural aspects of the child's country of origin, including books, dolls, toys, museum exhibits, music, and even visits to that country. Others don't believe this is necessary or important. This is another decision that you would need to make for your family.

Reality #5: Long-Term Institutionalization Does Affect Children

Study after study has documented that long-term living in an orphanage (even as short as eight or nine months for an infant or small child) can be devastating to the child's development and have far-reaching effects.

One study of "late-adopted" children from Romania compared those who had resided in an orphanage for over eight months to those who were adopted by age four months. The children who spent more time in the orphanage experienced more behavioral problems and were more likely to engage in autistic-like self-stimulating behaviors such as constant rocking.

Follow-ups as long as three years later indicated problems had improved but still existed. Many children adopted as older babies were more likely to be withdrawn or depressed than were the early adopted children.

Dr. Michael Rutter, a British physician, is studying the largest single group of Romanian children adopted from orphanages—166 children who were adopted by families in the United Kingdom. Some lived in an orphanage as long as eighteen months. He found great improvements in the children, but noted that they still lagged behind other children.

If you are considering adopting a child older than four to six months who has been raised in an orphanage, remember that although affection and attention can help a child achieve milestones, love does *not* conquer all. Before you adopt a child from a foreign orphanage, learn as much as you can about conditions in the orphanage, the age of the child, and any pertinent medical information.

TRAVELING TO A FOREIGN COUNTRY

Many countries that allow placement of children into the United States require that the adoptive parents travel to the country and comply with various rules and regulations. This can be a rather daunting requirement if you have never left the United States before, but good advance preparation should alleviate many of your anxieties. Most people advise that you should not travel alone, that you should travel with another adult so you will have emotional support while in a foreign land.

ADOPTING SIBLINGS
FROM ANOTHER COUNTRY

Some families choose to adopt two or more children from a country at a time because they do not want to separate siblings. It's always a good idea to at least ask the orphanage or agency if the child you intend to adopt has any siblings, and if so, what is their status. Even if you are unable to adopt the siblings, you can at least someday provide your adopted child with this information.

Although two children are more than "double trouble"—most parents will tell you that with each child, the workload increases exponentially—the reward may be that the child has the opportunity to grow up with a biological sibling. (Don't expect much gratitude—if any—as they grow up! Children fight and argue.)

Studies indicate that the outcomes of internationally adopted siblings are generally successful; however, the decision whether to parent more than one child must be made by *you* alone and should not be driven by any sense of guilt. Do not allow a social worker, orphanage director, or anyone else to talk you into adopting siblings unless you truly wish to do so.

Researchers have found that most adoptive parents of sibling groups were childless couples. They adopted more than one child because they planned on more than one child in their family and they also wanted to keep siblings together. They also believed that being with a sibling would be easier on both children than being adopted alone.

Of course, there are disadvantages to adopting siblings. Older children can sometimes be abusive to younger children, and there may also be an unhealthy interdependence between an older child and a younger one. This interdependence may be based in the past and may have developed out of necessity. In any case, the adoptive parents may find it hard to break through to assume their role as parents.

RESOURCES
ON INTERNATIONAL ADOPTION

One book with a workbook approach is *How to Adopt Internationally* by Jean Nelson-Erichsen (Mesa House Publishing, 1701 River Run Road, Suite 802, Ft. Worth, TX 76107; tel: 817-339-8889).

Another good source is *Report on Intercountry Adoption*, which is updated annually and offers ten updates per year. This book has information on adoption agencies nationwide as well as essays on adoption. It is published by International Concerns for Children, 911 Cyprus Drive, Boulder, CO, 80303-2821 ($20).

14

ADOPTING TRANSRACIALLY FROM THE UNITED STATES AND FROM OVERSEAS

Race should not matter, should it? Children are children. But, sadly, race still does matter in our culture today and if you are considering adopting a child of racial or ethnic heritage that is different from yours, your family will be affected. There are still bigoted people who make racial slurs and judge people solely by the color of their skin. If you adopt a child out of your race, then you too are considered a problem by such people. Your whole family will be affected—you, your spouse, if you are married, any siblings the child may have, and, of course, the adopted child.

Most people who adopt transracially are white because there are many African American and biracial babies and children who need families. Of course, blacks adopt children, but virtually all blacks adopt within their race. If there were a large number of white children who needed families, then blacks might consider adopting transracially. That is not the case. I have known blacks in the military who have adopted out of their race, such as a black officer and his wife who adopted an Asian orphan, but few do so.

WHEN YOU ADOPT TRANSRACIALLY, YOUR FAMILY IS SEEN AS A MINORITY FAMILY

If you are a white person who adopts a child who is black or biracial, then your family typically becomes viewed as a minority family, according to anecdotal reports from many social workers and adoptive

135

families. The public usually takes little notice of a white adult with a white child. Similarly, it's not unusual to see an African American child with an African American adult.

But if a white person with an African American child is noticed by many people, as would a black person with a white child be noticed. Some white parents of adopted black children have reported that they were asked by strangers if the child's father was black or if the child is a foster child or an adopted child.

An article in *Report on Intercountry Foreign Adoption 1997* offered these statements about transracial adoption: "Your family will now be interracial for generations. It is not just a question of an appealing little baby. How do you think and feel about interracial marriage? How does your family think and feel when people assume that you are married to an Oriental, a Spaniard, or a Black? How do you think and feel about getting some public attention—positive and negative stares, comments? A possible problem could be that the adopted child gets too much attention and others in the family tend to get 'left out.' "

If you think you would find it very difficult to deal with such issues, you should think hard before committing to adopting a child of another race.

However, there is an exception to transracial racism: A white person who adopts an Asian child is generally not recategorized as a member of a minority family. For the moment, Chinese, Korean, and other Asian children are generally seen in a positive light by most Americans. I cannot explain why this is the case, but it is true.

Do not interpret the preceding paragraphs to mean that I oppose transracial adoption—I do not. Too many children of minority races and ethnic backgrounds languish in foster care and are not adopted by black or other minority families. They could be adopted by white families if barriers that now exist in public agencies were removed. Children grow quickly, and they should not have to wait years for parents.

STUDIES SUPPORT
TRANSRACIAL ADOPTION

Studies done over time (longitudinal studies) by researchers such as Rita Simon and Howard Altstein have indicated that most transracial adoptions have good outcomes. Other studies also support this research (see *The Encyclopedia of Adoption* for further information). Of course, the older the child is at the age of adoption, the higher the probability of possible problems ahead. This is true no matter what the race of the child.

Many studies have been done on black and Korean children who were adopted by whites. Most of the children have adjusted well to their lives and have grown up with a higher socioeconomic level and probably a better overall life than if they had not been adopted, often exceeding the success of their biological siblings.

I see transracial adoption as a positive option, *if* the adoptive parents are ready for and accepting of the down side—the mostly negative reaction from society.

ORGANIZED OPPOSITION TO TRANSRACIAL ADOPTION

Some organizations are opposed to people adopting outside their own race. Most notably, the National Association of Black Social Workers has vocally opposed transracial adoption for over twenty years.

An article in a 1995 issue of *Public Welfare*, a publication targeted to state and county social workers, revealed the results of a study on the opinions of over two thousand child welfare administrators nationwide. The majority of social workers believed that race should be very important in adoptive placements. This was in the wake of the federal Multi-Ethnic Placement Act, passed in 1994, which forbade denials or delays in adoptive placements because of race.

But sentiment that is strongly entrenched does not change overnight. Even among social service administrators who were willing to consider transracial placements, some had misgivings. One person said, "Placement with adoptive homes that are not of a particular race denies that child of their cultural inheritance, unless the adoptive family commits to living, worshiping, shopping, in a race-appropriate neighborhood." The research supporting transracial adoption doesn't appear to move this view.

RACE AS A "SPECIAL NEED"

One fact that surprises many people is that infants and children who are not Caucasian are often considered to have "special needs" by virtue of race alone. So healthy black infants are said to have "special needs." Agencies and attorneys use this nomenclature because they often find it difficult to place black babies and children into adoptive families, many of whom are white and are seeking same-race children. In these cases, many adoption agencies drop the adoption fees. Consequently, some people then conclude, mistakenly, that agencies believe that non-white children aren't "worth" as much as white children and that they must be somehow second class. Healthy white infants are rarely designated as children with special needs. (Some circumstances might cause the agency to apply such a designation; for example, if the birthmother was a drug addict, or she was raped, or she was a victim of incest, etc.)

Because fewer people seek to adopt nonwhite children in the United States (and also because they are often tacitly discouraged from doing so by social workers), the agency may have no prospective adoptive parents on its list when a black birthmother comes in and wants to place her baby for adoption. Mothers often wait until the last trimester and sometimes until the final weeks of pregnancy to make the adoption choice. So there isn't much time.

When adoption agencies charge lower fees for a nonwhite child with special needs, they do so to facilitate an adoption and *not* because they believe the child is somehow not as valued as a healthy white child. The painful fact is that if agencies charged the same fees for children of color as they charge for white children, they would place even fewer of them in adoptive homes.

ATTITUDES OF OTHERS

You may think you already know how your friends and family would react if you adopted a child of another race. But you could be wrong. Some families have had to cut back or eliminate family visits because other family members refused to accept the adopted child. This can be very painful for all concerned, and it's especially hard for the child—she or he will soon realize why grandparents or aunts and uncles never visit.

But most important, consider the people in your own nuclear family—your spouse, any other children, and other people living in your household. What do they think about a transracial adoption? Even if you ask them what they think, they may not give you a straight answer. In some cases, they don't really know how they feel about it. It may never have occurred to them to wonder what it would be like to live with a person of another racial background.

Douglas Donnelly, an attorney from Santa Barbara, California, thinks it's especially important for prospective parents to tell the extended family if they are considering adopting a child of another race or of mixed race. Donnelly had one family who was very eager to adopt a biracial child, and he urged them to let family members know. "They consulted with the extended families and they went berserk. So the couple asked what to do, and I said I didn't think it would be fair to the child to be placed in their home. It's not the child's task to teach those people to be accepting of other races." The couple did not adopt the child.

QUESTIONS TO ASK YOURSELF

If you are considering transracial adoption, ask yourself these questions:

- Do you have any friends who are members of the child's race?
- Do you know what the racial or ethnic stereotypes are regarding this race? Do you ascribe to any of these stereotypes?
- If family members openly disapprove, would you be able to see them less frequently—or not at all—if that would be better for your child?
- Imagine your transracially adopted child as an adult. What sort of person would he or she be likely to marry?
- Are there any people of the child's race or ethnic group in your neighborhood, club, or faith group? If not, would you be willing to move if it might help the child?
- How would you help your child deal with teasing and taunting?

As you can see, there are many issues to consider when you are deciding not only if you should adopt but also if you should adopt a child of another race. As with other adoption issues, self-education and self-evaluation are really critical to making the best decision.

15

ADOPTING CHILDREN WITH "SPECIAL NEEDS"

Transracial adoption (see Chapter 14) is one category of "special need." But when most people think of special needs, they think of American children with medical, emotional, or psychiatric problems—all of which may be correctable or may be severe and lifelong.

Children from other countries may also have special needs; however, agencies or orphanages may exaggerate or underemphasize a child's medical problem. Obtain as much advance information as you can about the child, and, whenever possible, get a videotape of the child as well as a written description to show a physician in the United States.

WHAT SPECIAL NEEDS CAN YOU DEAL WITH?

A social worker recently told me that several of her adoptive parents were adopting children from other countries with serious heart problems. The children would need surgery almost immediately upon admission into the United States. These families had accepted the problem and were ready to deal with it. But many other far less serious medical problems are also classified as special needs.

One downside of adopting an older child with physical or emotional problems is that you may not get much sympathy if you ever complain about the child's problems. Jane reported that others said to her, "You didn't have to adopt her. You chose that course yourself." Jane wonders aloud if people would be more sympathetic had her child been born to her. She doubts that they would say, "You didn't have to have that baby. You chose to have her."

THE SPECIAL NEEDS CHECKLIST

Many couples are somewhat aghast when they apply to an adoption agency and are given a list of medical problems to which they must indicate their level of acceptance as yes, no, or maybe. Often, they have never considered this issue, having always assumed that the child would be perfectly healthy. In addition, what an agency considers a special need may not seem like a problem at all to an adoptive couple.

Bob and Cindy adopted a very healthy child who had a large birthmark on his back. The child was considered to have a special need by the agency because of his birthmark. The birthmark didn't bother Bob and Cindy when they adopted their son, and it still doesn't bother them.

What is considered a special need also varies from agency to agency. In one agency, only children who have severe disabilities may be considered to have special needs; whereas in another, which concentrates on placing healthy infants, even a minor problem could be construed as a special need. It's always a good idea to ask the agency to define its terms.

WHO ADOPTS CHILDREN
WITH SPECIAL NEEDS?

People who adopt children with special needs are often couples in their late thirties or forties (older than most baby adopters), and in many cases, these couples already have children—sometimes adult children. Adoptive parents who seem to do the best with children with special needs are those who are flexible and adaptable and count meeting the child's needs as most important.

Sometimes the adoptive parents themselves have the same or similar special need as the children they adopt. For example, Fred chose not to have biological children because he had a rare genetic disease that prevented him from sweating and that required him to live in a cold climate. He did not want to pass on this problem to biological children. Fred and his wife adopted three children from Asia who have the same illness as Fred. He reasoned that he knew how to deal with the problem better than anyone else, and he knew that it would be hard for the children to find other families.

In another case, attorney Douglas Donnelly was preparing to place a child when the ultrasound of the unborn baby revealed that the child was a dwarf. The prospective parents absolutely refused to adopt the child, so Donnelly found another family through the adoption coordinator for the Little People of America. He received five resumes from dwarf couples, and the birthmother chose one of the families.

ADOPTING FOSTER CHILDREN

All states place foster children for adoption, although in most cases these are older children. The parental rights of the children have usually been involuntarily terminated because of abuse, neglect, or abandonment, and often the children have been in foster care for years or most of their lives.

Sometimes the children have been in a revolving-door pattern—in foster care; then back to the parent, where they are abused again; then back in foster care, and so on. State social workers have been mandated to try to place a child back with a biological family whenever possible. Many judges keep children in the foster care limbo, not understanding the damage it does to a child to stay in this system for years.

The advantages of adopting a foster child are that the adoptive parents pay no fees and the child may be eligible to continue to receive Medicaid health insurance. And these are children who truly need parents.

The disadvantages lie primarily in parenting a child who may have faced severe physical or emotional abuse in the past. Studies reveal that foster children often receive very poor health care or none at all while in foster care—often their health care has been worse than the care received by people who are homeless. As a result, the child may have major or minor physical problems that need immediate attention. The child may need glasses, and he or she will probably need dental care.

ADOPTING ABUSED CHILDREN

Children who are known to have been abused are usually categorized as having special needs. In many cases, abused children from the United States are placed by state or county agencies.

The abuse could have been physical, emotional, or sexual—or all three. Physical abuse can take many forms, such as beatings or starving, and may have caused temporary or permanent physical harm. A child could have been subjected to constant screaming, threatening, and demeaning behavior, although this type of emotional abuse is not enough by itself to place a child in foster care. Physical and/or sexual abuse are the usual reasons for removal to foster care.

Sexual abuse could mean that the child was exposed to the sexual behavior of others in the family, or that the child was sexually stimulated or even forced to engage in sexual intercourse. The sexual behavior could have been incestuous. A child who has continually been sexually abused could see such behavior as being normal, despite what others have told him or her. Thus, masturbating in public or attempting to seduce an adult is not uncommon behavior in sexually abused children.

The adoptive parent needs considerable patience and restraint in dealing with a sexually abused child and in helping him or her to learn appropriate behavior. The older the child, the more difficult it is to cope with the child. Adolescents are the most challenging of all. Girls who have been sexually abused and are adopted from foster care seem to present some of the most difficult problems and appear to be far more sexually aggressive than girls in the general population.

Foster children sometimes display types of mental illness as well, and there are indicators of increased psychopathology in foster children versus the general population. This further complicates the parenting of a sexually abused child. Despite having normal intelligence, many children who have been sexually abused experience school difficulties, academic delays, and other problems.

ADOPTING CHILDREN
WITH MEDICAL PROBLEMS

Medical problems of a child to be adopted may be minor and correctable or may range all the way to severe and life-threatening. For example, a newborn child might have a hernia, which can be resolved by surgery, or he or she might have Down's syndrome.

Obviously, children who test HIV positive are considered to have a special need. However, an infant may test positive because of the mother's antibodies, and it is possible (and likely) that the child could "convert" to normal.

Fetal alcohol syndrome (FAS) is another problem faced by some children. FAS is a complicated series of neurological and physical problems that have directly resulted from the biological mother's abuse of alcohol during her pregnancy. Often the child is of below-normal intelligence; thus, the prospective parent who values normal or above-average intelligence is not a good candidate to adopt a child with FAS (or a child with Down's syndrome).

ADOPTING SCHOOL-AGE CHILDREN

Charlotte Lopez, former Miss Teenage America, was adopted in Vermont when she was nearly eighteen years old, after having been raised in foster care most of her life. The state of Vermont removed Lopez several times from her mentally ill and abusive mother, and she ultimately remained "in the system" from about the age of three. Lopez was fortunate in that she and her sister were able to live with one foster family until Charlotte was about sixteen. The state terminated the parental rights of their mother, but the foster parents never adopted the girls.

Lopez developed a tumultuous relationship with her strict foster parents and was placed in a group home. At age sixteen, she verbalized her lifelong desire for an adoptive family and pressed her social workers to find her such a family. They did.

Lopez won the Miss Teenage America contest and said, "I thought it was the moment of my greatest victory. But it was not. That came some months later, on March 7, 1994, when Jill and Al adopted me and became my parents."

Lopez is now a college student and author of *Lost in the System.*

Most school-age children available for adoption are foster children from the United States or children from other countries. Many have had very poor health care. They may also suffer from a variety of emotional problems related to abuse, neglect, and abandonment. Many experts say that it is realistic to assume that every child in foster care has been abused and to proceed accordingly. The child may also exhibit behavioral problems, either because of early negative environments or inherited problems or both.

Many times, social service agencies seek to place groups of siblings together. If you have had no experience with children, think hard before adopting two or more older siblings. Many people who adopt older foster children have already parented other children and are somewhat better prepared to care for these children.

You should not expect a ten-year-old who has been in foster care for five years to act the same way as the ten-year-old next door who has lived in an intact family all his life.

Adopted kids may be suspicious or frightened or happy and excited, but don't expect them to be "grateful" to be adopted. Gratitude doesn't come with parenthood.

Despite all of the rather negative aspects of adopting older children, many people have successfully adopted older kids and formed very happy loving families. You may decide that it's the right path for you as well.

ADOPTING SIBLING GROUPS

Unless they are healthy newborn twins, virtually every group of two or more children is considered to have special needs. It is hard to recruit a suitable family that is willing to take more than one child, even if the children are healthy. But I have known families who have adopted four children or five children at a time—a challenging course of action and a major change in their lives!

Often siblings have formed their own interrelationships before becoming part of your family; for example, one child may have taken on a maternal or paternal role toward the others and be reluctant to give this role up to the authority of adults.

GET AS MUCH INFORMATION
AS YOU CAN

If you are thinking about adopting a child with special needs, you should be sure to obtain a clear and written definition from the agency on the child's special needs. Do not allow yourself to be pressured into adopting a child with special needs because "the poor child won't have a family otherwise." Most agencies do not use such tactics, but some do. Many children in the United States and abroad need families, and you do not do a child a favor by adopting solely out of pressure or pity.

QUESTIONS TO ASK YOURSELF

Here are a few questions you might consider before adopting children with special medical needs. You don't have to know all the answers now about how to solve all problems that might come up. The main point is, Are you willing and able to solve them or work on them? If so, and if you want to adopt a child with special needs, then you may find your life to be very fulfilled, as have many before you.

- Do you have good medical coverage? Most insurance policies must now cover adopted children. But if the child needs psycho-therapy and that is not offered in your plan, then you would have to pick up the bill unless the foster child's Medicaid coverage continues and includes psychotherapy.
- If the child needed special medical care that is unavailable where you live, would you be willing to move?
- If the child needed modifications or extra help in school, would you be willing to act as advocate?
- Could the child go on vacation with you, or would you need to forego vacations for a while?
- Suppose the child has medical problems. Do you mind being around hospitals and/or doctors?
- Would you be able to cope with a child whose special need was psychological?
- How would you help the child deal with a disability?

16

OPEN ADOPTION

One of the toughest aspects of open adoption is figuring out what it is! I define open adoption as a complete sharing of identities—the adoptive parents and birthparents know each other's first *and* last names. Other people define open adoption as the exchanging of non-identifying information or a one-time meeting on a first-name basis only. The only way to really know what open adoption means to an agency or attorney is to ask for an explanation and a definition.

UNDERSTANDING OPEN ADOPTION

Both ignorance and fear have probably prevented many people from adopting. Maybe you want a confidential adoption, but you feel that it just cannot be done today. So you never pursue adopting a child at all. Or perhaps you *do* want information about birthparents and think that you cannot obtain it. Do not assume. Get the facts.

Although the trend today appears to lean toward "semi-open" adoptions, those in which limited information is shared and meetings are arranged and letters are exchanged through an intermediary, this is not the only way to adopt. If you search, you can usually find the agency or attorney that will provide the level of openness or confidentiality that suits your family.

ONLY AGREE TO WHAT YOU CAN LIVE WITH

As prospective adoptive parents, you should *not* agree to anything that you don't feel you can live with later. And if you do agree to provide pictures or letters once a year or to do something else, then follow through. "It's very important that whatever agreement they have made with the birthparents, that they should stick with it," says attorney Mary Ann Scherer of Fort Lauderdale. "We see the tears of the birthmother later on if they don't. We get signed agreements, but it's still a good-faith thing since consent in Florida can't be conditional."

Scherer often sees reluctant compliance. "We see pictures where the baby is all scrunched up and poor quality pictures sometimes. Don't send the pictures with the red eyes, where the child is unsmiling! Don't send a picture [taken from] so far away that you can't even see that this is a child!" Scherer says most adoptive parents do fulfill their agreements. She also notes that often the birthmother goes on with her life and only needs the pictures or letters for a year or two as a sort of cushion to ensure that the child is well and happy.

Douglas Donnelly, an attorney from Santa Barbara, says that he does open adoptions that are generally very intense relationships between the birthparents and adoptive parents at the time of delivery. After that, the adoptive family usually sends letters and pictures to the birthmother for about two years. Later, they send the letters and pictures to him or to an intermediary in case the birthmother wants them. (Donnelly notes that every adoption is different, and it is definitely not a one-size-fits-all experience for his clients.)

IS OPEN ADOPTION GOOD FOR BIRTHMOTHERS?

Many agencies and attorneys assume that an open adoption must be good for a birthmother, because this way she can meet prospective parents and have a choice in who adopts her child. Why should someone who is thinking about adopting care if open adoption is good or bad for birthmothers? Because open adoption is often promoted to prospective adoptive parents as an option that is better and more fair for the birthmother.

Some studies support the view that birthmothers are happier with an open adoption; some dispute it. One study published in 1990 in *Child Welfare* found that birthmothers who placed their infants in an open adoption experienced more grief, as measured in a modified Grief Experience Inventory, than did birthmothers who placed in a confidential adoption.

Interestingly, on the surface, the birthmothers who placed their children in an open adoption had adjusted better: Nearly 78 percent of the open adoption group expressed positive emotions versus 56 percent of the confidential group. But when the birthmothers took the Grief Inventory, the open adoption birthmothers scored significantly higher levels of problem symptoms than the norm on eight bereavement sub-scales: social isolation, sleep disturbance, optimism versus despair, somaticizing (developing physical symptoms of illness because you are so upset), appetite, vigor, physical symptoms, and dependency.

The confidential birthmothers scored higher than the norm on four scales: sleep disturbance, loss of appetite, loss of vigor, and optimism versus despair.

The researchers concluded that the experience was more difficult for the open adoption birthmothers: "It might seem a paradox that continued knowledge about the relinquished child would intensify a mother's grief symptoms. A similar grief pattern appears, however, among divorced women who often have a harder time letting go and recovering emotionally than do widows. Death of a partner appears to be almost freeing in its finality and seldom promotes self-blame or fantasies of reunion."

Of course, the researchers are not saying that it would be better if the child were dead; they are simply providing an analogy to explain why and how open adoption could be a difficult experience. Perhaps years later, the open adoption birthmothers will be faring much better than the confidential adoption birthmothers.

Other studies have found that adoption that offers the birth-mother choices is a much better experience for birthmothers. For example, a study of Canadian birthmothers reported in a 1996 issue of *Child Welfare* found that birthmothers were far more able to deal with the adoption decision when they had met and chosen the adoptive parents. These birthmothers did not have an ongoing relationship with the adopted child. The researchers also found that birthmothers who had minimal contact with the child after birth were more likely to proceed with the adoption plan.

IS OPEN ADOPTION GOOD FOR ADOPTIVE PARENTS AND ADOPTED KIDS?

This is a tough question to answer, and you should consider it carefully. Ask social workers who talk to you about open adoption to give their opinion. On the plus side, if you know the identity of the birthmother or if you could readily contact her, either directly or through the agency, then she's accessible if you need her or want to speak to her. And if your child ever wants to contact his or her birthmother, there will be no need to spend months or years trying to track her down.

Proponents also say that open adoption is an "honest" and good way to proceed. They believe that confidential adoption is a problem because of the inherent secrecy.

Dissenters say that some birthmothers exhibit problem behavior and might want to have more contact with you and the child than you feel comfortable with. They believe that adoptive parents might have entitlement problems if the birthmother is regularly part of the child's life. (Proponents, however, say that the birthmother is often treated similarly to an aunt or a cousin.)

It's not possible to address all the issues in one section of this book; however, there are many pros and cons to consider and numerous questions to ask if you are considering either an open or a confidential adoption. Ask the questions.

MORE RESEARCH IS NEEDED

Numerous studies support or refute open adoption as the right path to follow, and probably more studies support it than refute it. Personally, I would like to see a study that compares (1) birthmothers who have continuing relationships with the adoptive families and children to (2) birthmothers who met only before the adoption and may have exchanged letters and pictures, and that compares those results to (3) birthmothers whose adoptions were completely confidential. I would also like to see researchers take a look at the psychological well-being of the children themselves. I think that data from such a study would be fascinating and useful.

YOUR FAMILY MAY OBJECT TO OPEN ADOPTION

If you choose to adopt in an open or semi-open adoption (with some involvement of the birthmother—perhaps meeting on a first-name basis), your family may become hysterical. They are afraid and they are protective.

"The family doesn't understand it and they are afraid of open adoption," says Maxine Chalker, executive director of Adoptions From the Heart. Chalker has given seminars to extended family members so that they too can understand the ins and outs of open adoption.

The bottom line is that if you feel open adoption is right for you, then your family will need to learn to accept your decision. Or, if your family is adamantly opposed to an open adoption and you feel that your relationship with them would be impaired if you follow this course, you may need to rethink your decision.

QUESTIONS TO ASK YOURSELF ABOUT OPEN ADOPTION

There are many issues involved with open adoption, too many to cover in this volume. But at least ask yourself these questions:

- Are you agreeing to "openness" primarily because you are in a hurry to adopt a child, any child?
- Have you imagined yourself fulfilling the requests of the birthmother? For example, if she wants photos each year, will you willingly comply or do you think it might become a problem for you when your child is five years old or ten years old?
- If the birthmother wants more contact or less contact than originally agreed, will you be able to deal with this?
- Is the agency or attorney willing to serve as an intermediary, or would you prefer direct contact?

The proponents of open adoption insist that it's the one and only right way to manage an adoption. You may find that being chosen by a birthmother as *the* parent(s) to her child is an extremely positive and validating experience. However, if you believe that a confidential adoption would be better for your situation, you can still find many agencies and attorneys who can assist you.

Do *not* make your decision for or against open adoption based on what you've read here. Read more, talk to others, and learn as much as you can before deciding.

17

COMMENTS FROM PEOPLE WHO CONSIDERED ADOPTION

In this chapter are the perspectives of various people who have considered adoption. Some did adopt; others decided that adoption was not right for them. Their reasons, pro and con, are described in this chapter. In addition, I also asked the adoptive parents what, if anything, they would do differently today.

REASONS WHY SOME CHOSE ADOPTION

Most adopters had initial reservations about adoption, but their intense desire to become parents overcame their fears and they actively pursued adoption.

"We spent nearly two years in fertility treatment, and when faced with the option of moving to high-tech fertility treatment, decided that the odds of becoming a parent were much higher through adoption than through IVF [in vitro fertilization]," explained Darlene. "We were attracted to adoption by the fact that we would hold our child in our arms eventually, without any further medical tests or treatment. The infertility struggle caused us to lose sight of our goal—to become parents! Stepping off the medical treadmill was the best thing that we ever did—it restored our sanity and got us onto the right track."

Other parents echoed the view that they wanted to become parents, first and foremost. Said Jim, "Rather than waste time and money on something with no guarantees (drugs, surgery, IVF, etc.), we knew that if we worked at it and just hung in, we would have our dream come true."

Said Jennifer, "Having a family is the important thing, not how that family was formed. Love, not biology, is what truly makes a family."

Of course, there were doubts and fears among the adopters. Andrea recalls her primary fear: "We knew that birthmothers could change their minds and this was right around the time of Baby Jessica! [A child who was placed back with her biological parents in a controversial court case.] That was scary!"

REASONS WHY SOME DECIDED
NOT TO ADOPT

In general, non-adopters said that they believed the process was too difficult and the cost was just too high. In many cases, they were influenced by problems that friends had—or that they perceived their friends were having—with adoption.

Mona feels confident she made the right decision. "We recently inherited some money that would have allowed us to do a foreign adoption, but we have a friend going through the procedure right now. Although it supposedly will be a sure thing, she's been put through the wringer with reams of paperwork, information needed that was not made clear initially, unexpected problems, and months of waiting. We decided to buy a house in a great neighborhood that is convenient to our work and has everything we will want for years to come. If we had children, we would never be able to afford this house or this neighborhood, so in the end, we went for the sure bet."

Mona added that she loves her dream house, she loves traveling, and she is comfortable with her decision. "I love going home to my nice quiet house with white carpets!" she says.

Betty said that she has investigated international adoption but was put off by the expense and also by the time involved in traveling to a foreign country. She just did not want to leave her job for that long.

Sandy was a social worker at an adoption agency and yet she decided against adoption. She felt the process was too emotionally draining and did not want to become part of it. Her husband was also negative about the idea. But giving up the idea of adoption has not been an easy decision for her. Sandy explained, "The hardest part about deciding to remove adoption as an option is that I continually battle my head with my heart. I am in a nurturing profession and would like to have a child to raise. But my head tells me otherwise." She advises others, "Find support from other adopters and educate yourself as much as possible before you commit yourself."

Several people felt very damaged by their own infertility, to the extent that they felt "defective." Denise has been pregnant three times, and each time lost the baby. She said, "So far, there is no real reason why I can't get and stay pregnant. So I feel as if I would have to be totally ready to give up the dream of carrying a baby before I could consider adopting. Once you've been pregnant and lost the child, I think the need to have a successful pregnancy grows stronger. You know the joy of a positive test, the joy of watching your body change, and then the intense loneliness of day by day watching those things slip away when the baby dies . . . I want to be a parent, but I feel if I can't do it at least once on my own, maybe there is something about me that just isn't good enough."

WHAT ADOPTERS SAY THEY WOULD HAVE DONE DIFFERENTLY

Knowing what they know now about adoption, would the adoptive parents have handled things any differently? "I would have read more, and joined a support group earlier," said Lori. "I would have talked to more people, and let everyone know of my plans. Most of all, I would have talked to others who had adopted successfully, as well as with others at the same stages as me." Lori believes that if she had shared her desire to adopt with others, she would have received the information and support that she needed.

Lori also advises those who are undecided to talk with people who have adopted *and* with people who have chosen to not adopt or bear children, in order to weigh the options.

Lori adds, "I would urge anyone to enjoy life as a non-parent for the time being, and to prepare mentally for a whole new life. I believe that there is a baby for every family and it's just a matter of the two coming together. Adoption takes a lot: time, money, hard work, patience, perseverance, understanding, and a sense of humor. And that's just for starters! But I always tell people that if they are serious, willing to work at it and not just wait for the phone to ring, it's not a matter of *if*, it's a matter of *when* they will become parents."

18

BASIC POINTERS
FOR THOSE WHO
DECIDE TO ADOPT

M ost adoption books are dedicated to the how-tos of adoption or to parenting a child or to other related goals. My mission has been to help you decide whether or not adoption would be right for you. This chapter offers some final suggestions for those of you who have decided that adoption is the right answer, and it provides some basic information you'll need.

FINDING A GOOD
ADOPTION AGENCY

Here are several main points to consider in order to locate a good agency:

- Some adoption agencies do not advertise. Some are new and may not yet have ads in your Yellow Pages. Some do not believe in advertising. (However, if an agency does not believe in advertising, birthmothers probably do not know it exists.)
- Agencies are very different. Some emphasize religion, others concentrate on international adoption, and still others believe that open adoption is the most important part of their mission.
- Some agencies have an orientation program that prospective adoptive parents can attend free of charge. The program gives you an opportunity to learn about the policies and ask questions in person. If you go to the orientation and are pressured to apply, resist. Go home and think about it first.

- Ask people in adoptive parent groups what they think of the agency. Keep in mind that people who adopted through this agency are often inclined to be too positive. Others may repeat untrue gossip. Listen carefully and take all advice and information with the proverbial grain of salt.
- Ask for and review fee schedules. Add up the various charges before you do comparisons, and also understand what services are being supplied. There is a wide variation in fees for adoption.
- Do not assume that the agency that charges the most is the best agency. Of course, it could be the best—or it could be worst. Fees may have nothing to do with the quality of services.
- Contact the National Council For Adoption and ask them for their Hotline packets on choosing an agency or attorney.

FINDING A GOOD
ADOPTION ATTORNEY

If you choose to adopt independently—that is, adopting without using an agency—you may need an adoption attorney to help you. In some states, adoption attorneys can identify birthmothers who are seeking families for their children and can handle the entire adoption. In other states, prospective adoptive parents and birthmothers must find each other, often through networking or advertising.

Whether the attorney's role is minimal or paramount, be sure that he or she is experienced and ethical. Some attorneys limit their practices to adoptions only; others handle a variety of legal matters, usually family law cases. Here are some tips for seeking a good attorney:

- Seek information about the attorney from adoptive parent groups located in the area where the attorney practices. If the attorney is located out of your state, ask an adoptive parent group in the attorney's state. It could be well worth the toll call to obtain this information. If the person you contact sounds hesitant, it could mean either that he or she does not know much about the particular attorney or that he or she doesn't like the attorney but is afraid to say so. If you aren't sure, say something like, "Has anyone you know had any dealings with this attorney? Is he basically unfamiliar to you or do you know of him?"

- The American Academy of Adoption Attorneys is a national organization with hundreds of members, and you can contact them to find members in your state. There are good adoption attorneys, however, who are not yet members of the academy, for whatever reason. Nonmembership in the academy is not necessarily bad—and membership is not necessarily an indication of excellence.
- Once you have names of some attorneys, call and ask to speak briefly with them on the phone. (Don't take more than five or ten minutes.) Ask the attorney if he or she handles adoptions, and if so, about how many has he or she been involved with? How many were in the past year? Is she or he interested in new prospective adoptive parents? If so, ask if she or he would be willing to meet with you, and find out how much that would cost. (Don't expect the first meeting to be free, although it may be.)

If you decide you wish to work with a particular attorney, you may be asked for a retainer, a fee that may be set aside in a bank account to be used when adoption fees come up. The attorney should tell you how much of a retainer is needed and should outline the total costs, with a range of high to low. He or she should also give you a contract to sign. Read it carefully and ask any questions you have *before* signing it.

SCREENING REQUIREMENTS

Some agencies and attorneys require psychological screening of prospective parents. Mary Ann Scherer, an attorney in Fort Lauderdale, Florida, who has required a psychological evaluation of all prospective adoptive parents for nearly twenty years, says, "I have a clinical psychologist give me a report, based on the testing and the interviews, on the suitability of the prospective parents for adoption. I have picked up maybe six serious problems in all these years—but a child was not jeopardized as a result in those six cases."

Although you may approach such a screening with great trepidation, the purpose is to screen out people with severe emotional disorders who would have difficulty being a parent. You do not have to be perfect to obtain a "thumbs up" from a psychologist or therapist. Says Scherer, "We have a professional responsibility to the child and we can't minimize that."

The reason why you want to adopt will be explored. If you are infertile, you will be asked to explain the nature of the infertility, and you may be asked for verification. The reasons why you want to be a parent will be asked as well. (After reading through this book and considering the many aspects of parenting and adoption, you should feel ready to answer this line of questioning.)

MEDICAL ISSUES
IN ADOPTED CHILDREN

Medical topics related to adoption interest me, and I publish *Adoption/Medical News*, a newsletter with the latest information on medical issues of interest to agencies, support groups, adoptive parents, and others. Jerri Ann Jenista, M.D., a noted pediatrician with great expertise in this field, writes the articles for this publication. (It is published ten times a year for $36. A sample copy is available for $3. Write to Adoption Advocates Press, 1921 Ohio St. NE, Suite 5, Palm Bay, FL 32907.)

If you have decided to adopt an infant or older child from the United States, you may mistakenly assume that complete medical records are readily available. This may be true if the child is an infant, and you should certainly seek the information; however, if the child is older, and particularly if the child is a foster child, medical records may be extremely sketchy. Here are some brief guidelines on what to look for if you are thinking about adopting a child from the United States, based on information provided by pediatrician Dr. Jerri Ann Jenista.

If the Child Is an Infant

• Obtain, or ask the agency or attorney to obtain, information on the health of birthparents and on any possible genetic conditions they may have. Whenever possible, obtain the same type of information on the parents of the birthparents, because birthparents are usually in their late teens or twenties and in good health, whereas problems that they may inherit are often already occurring in their own parents. Specifically ask about psychiatric illnesses, heart disease, diabetes, and other major illnesses.

- Make sure that the agency or attorney gets, in writing, information on the pregnancy and on the delivery. Be sure that information is sought on testing for HIV, syphilis, hepatitis B, and drugs.
- Ask the agency or attorney to obtain the discharge physical examination information on the baby from the hospital, and ask if there were any notes on possible unusual conditions seen then in the infant.
- Ask the agency or attorney to obtain the results of screenings done on the newborn.

If the Child Is an Older Child from the United States

- Ask for a record of all immunizations. If the medical record is incomplete or unavailable, the child's school probably has this information and the social worker can obtain it from this source.
- Ask for a medical history of the child and the family. If it is not in the record, ask the social worker to try to obtain more information.
- Find out about past serious illnesses and any allergies or drug reactions. Ask if the child has had any broken bones, scars, or other injuries.
- Request a copy of the discharge papers for every time the child has been hospitalized in the past, including psychiatric evaluations. (You may receive some resistance to this request, but press for it anyway!)
- Ask for any written evaluations by medical specialists.
- Request copies of Individualized Education Programs (IEPs). These are special plans written by the school and the parent or foster parent of the child.
- Request dental records.
- Ask for written information on past physical or sexual abuse.
- Consider HIV screening for the child, if sexual abuse or drug abuse may have occurred.

For All Children Adopted from Other Countries

Whether the child you adopt is an infant or an older child, gather the following information:

- Ask for the birth date of the child. If this is unknown, ask for an estimated date.
- Get the results of the last physical examination. According to pediatrician Jenista, if the child is under the age of one, make sure the information was within the last one to two months. If the child is under age five, make sure the information was within the last six months. For children over five, the information should be no older than one year. However, for the child who has a medical problem, regardless of his or her age, the physical examination should be data that is no more than two months old.
- Obtain the weight of the child.
- Ask for the head circumference of any child under the age of two. This information is very important to physicians and helps them evaluate a child's growth progress both in relation to other children and in relation to himself or herself over time.
- Ask for written results of the physical examination and for written information on any problems the doctor noted. If the information was written in another language, get it translated by someone who understands medical language. (Ask the agency or orphanage to assist you.)
- Obtain an evaluation of the child's physical and mental progress compared to other children in his or her own country. Remember, children from other countries are sometimes smaller than children from the United States. If the child was on-track for other children in her age group in her country, this is a good sign.
- Ask for any information on the pregnancy or delivery. Information may not be available, but ask anyway.
- Obtain a list of any hospitalizations or serious illnesses. Find out if the child has received (or is receiving) medication. Does the child have any known allergies or drug reactions?
- Ask for the dates of immunizations. Also, ask for the results of BCG vaccine for tuberculosis. Get the information in writing.
- Ask for lab test results.
- If there is a video on the child, get it! Ask a pediatrician to look at the video, keeping in mind that the child is from another country, to see if the child has any apparent problems.

When your child comes into this country, be sure that he or she obtains a complete medical screening. The following tests should be performed by your pediatrician:

- Complete blood count
- Urinalysis
- Hepatitis B serology
- VDRL or another syphilis test
- Mantoux (PPD) tuberculosis test. The skin prick test should *NOT* be used.
- Stool specimen test for parasites and ova. At least three samples should be provided—one is not enough.
- HIV screening. It does not matter if the child was tested in the other country. Retest.

CONCLUSION

Of course only *you* can make the decision about whether adoption would be right for you and your family. In this book, I've covered the primary myths and misconceptions and the many emotions involved with adopting a child, as well as how others may help or hinder you along the way. I've discussed infertility treatment and feelings about infertility, and I hope that you now have the insight to evaluate your own situation and determine whether to continue treatments or to stop. I also hope that you can now decide if what you really want is to adopt a child.

Whether adopted by you or born to you, children are not perfect, and neither are you or other family members. But you do need to have or develop patience, empathy, and other qualities discussed in this book. You also need to understand that adoption does not "end" when the baby is placed in your arms or when the older child enters your home. Issues will come up and people will ask questions, regardless of the child you adopt. The feelings and attitudes of your spouse about adoption are very important, and the feelings of your extended family can be very significant in how your life will change with an adopted child.

My mission with this book is not to send every reader off to the nearest adoption agency or lawyer. If, after reading this book, you decide that you don't want to adopt, that is okay! And if your decision is to adopt, that is okay, too. My goal is to help you educate and evaluate yourself. Whatever your decision about adoption, my best wishes go with you.

APPENDIX A
BAD AND GOOD REASONS TO ADOPT

Bad Reasons

You want to save your marriage.

You're bored.

You want your partner to be happy, but you don't want to adopt.

You want to save the world and to make a statement.

You want to "give" your child a sibling.

You want to replace a child who died.

You want to adopt an older child—around two—because you don't want to deal with messy diapers and late-night feedings. Older kids are easier.

Good Reasons

You have a good marriage and you want to be a parent.

Your life is mostly happy, but you feel parenthood would be fulfilling.

You both want to adopt.

You like children and want to create or expand your family by adopting.

Having a sibling will be an extra benefit for children you already have now—but that isn't your main reason to adopt.

No child can replace another. If or when you are ready to love another child for himself, then consider adoption. Otherwise, don't.

Many older children who need adoptive parents are over seven or eight years old. Few American birthmothers place their toddlers for adoption. Toddlers from foreign countries need parents—but don't expect them to behave just like your neighbor's two-year-old. The child also has many new things to get used to: language, customs, *YOU*.

169

Bad Reasons	*Good Reasons*
You want a school-age child so you can continue working.	The child over age two may have been abused and could face some problems and issues. Count on a few calls at work, and count on the child needing extra love and support at the beginning of your relationship.
You had a hysterectomy and you think adoption will help you get over the emotional pain.	Grieving can't be completely avoided without repercussions. Be fair to yourself and any children you adopt: wait until you're ready.
You are white and you have a black or Asian or other minority child. Therefore, you should adopt another one.	Closely related to the "give your child a sibling" reason, but with a racist tinge. Don't adopt another child, black, Asian, or otherwise, unless and until *you* feel ready.
You'll be regarded as being more responsible if you adopt.	You want to adopt because it feels right for your family.
You can avoid the difficulties of pregnancy. You can keep your good figure.	If pregnancy would be medically difficult for you and if you really want to be a parent, adoption may be the answer. But if your main reason is that you don't want to wreck your beautiful body with a pregnancy—you're not ready to adopt. Children need parents who place *them* very high in the priorities of life!
You think adoption will help your career.	You know children take time away from work, and you accept this.
People tell you that you'd made a great parent.	You feel that you'd be a good parent—and you *want* to be one.

Bad Reasons	*Good Reasons*
Those poor children need someone to give them a home. Adoption is better than an orphanage.	Children need a family that really wants them. Adoption is better than an orphanage *if* a child is truly wanted.
You want someone to take care of you when you're old.	Don't count on adult children caring for you in your old age! Instead, adopt children now to give them the good parenting and love they need and to gain the joys (and some tough times) of parenting.
You're lonely, and you need someone to love you. (This is the same reason why teenage girls who get pregnant decide to parent their babies. It doesn't work well for them either.)	You have a strong self-image, but you'd also like a child in your life. You feel that you can give as well as receive love.

APPENDIX B
RESOURCES FOR HELP AND INFORMATION

Recommended Publications

Adoptalk
North American Council on Adoptable
   Children (NACAC)
970 Raymond Ave., Ste. 106
St. Paul, MN 55114-1149
Tel: 612-644-3036
Quarterly publication devoted to
legislation, issues, and information
about children with special needs.

Adoption/Medical News
1921 Ohio St. NE
Palm Bay, FL 32907
A four-page newsletter written by
Jerri Ann Jenista, M.D. on medical
issues of interest to adoption
professionals, adoptive parent groups,
and others.
Ten issues, $36.
Tel: 407-724-0815

Adoptive Families
2309 Como Ave.
St. Paul, MN 55108
Tel: 1-800-372-3300 or 612-645-9955
Six issues, $24.95
Bimonthly magazine for adopting
and adoptive parents.

*The Handbook for Single
   Adoptive Parents*
A comprehensive guide on adopting for
   singles.
$20

*National Council for Single
   Adoptive Parents*
P.O. Box 150842
Chevy Chase, MD 20825

National Adoption Reports
National Council For Adoption
1930 Seventeenth St. N.W.
Washington, DC 20009
Tel: 202-328-1200
A monthly newsletter packed with the
latest news and information on adoption.
$24 subscription fees included in annual
membership of $50.

Report on Intercountry Adoption
International Concerns for Children
911 Cypress Dr.
Boulder, CO 80303-2821
Tel: 303-494-8333 (voice and fax)
e-mail: http://www.fortnet.org/icc
Important annual listing of the
latest information on international
adoption. Valuable for adopting
parents and adoption professionals.
Updated ten times per year. $20 per year.

ROOTS & WINGS
ROOTS & WINGS Publications
P.O. Box 577
Hackettstown, NJ 07840
Tel: 908-637-4259
e-mail: adoption@world2u.com
Internet web site:
   http://www.adopting.org/rw.html
Quarterly magazine with adoption
   articles. $19.95 per year.

National Organizations

Adoptive Families of America
2309 Como Ave.
St. Paul, MN 55108
Tel: 1-800-372-3300 or 612-645-9955

American Academy of Adoption
   Attorneys
P.O. Box 33053
Washington, DC 20033-0053
Tel: 202-832-2222

American Society for Reproductive
   Medicine
(formerly the American Fertility
   Society)
409 12th St. S.W., Ste. 203
Washington, DC 20024
Tel: 202-863-2439

Infertility Awareness Association of
   Canada
201–396 Cooper St.
Ottawa, Ontario K2P 2H7
Tel: 613-234-8585

International Concerns for Children
911 Cypress Dr.
Boulder, CO 80303
Tel: 303-494-8333
(Produces *Report on Intercountry
Adoption*; $20 including updates.)

National Adoption Information
   Clearinghouse (NAIC)
Caliber Associates
P.O. Box 1182
Washington, DC 20013
Tel: 888-251-0075 or 703-352-3488

National Council For Adoption
1930 Seventeenth St., N.W.
Washington, DC 20009
Tel: 202-328-1200

National Council for Single Adoptive
   Parents
P.O. Box 15084
Chevy Chase, MD 20825

North American Council on Adoptable
   Children (NACAC)
970 Raymond Ave., Ste. 106
St. Paul, MN 55114-1149
Tel: 612-644-3036

RESOLVE, Inc.
1310 Broadway
Somerville, MA 02144-1731
Helpline: 617-623-0744

Tapestry Books
P.O. Box 359
Ringoes, NJ 08551
Tel: 800-765-2367

State Adoption Units

Alabama
Alabama Office of Adoption
Department of Human Resources
50 N. Ripley St.
Montgomery, AL 36130
Tel: 205-242-9500

Alaska
Alaska Division of Family and Youth
   Services
Box 110630
Juneau, AK 99811-0630
Tel: 907-265-5080

Arizona
Arizona Department of Economic
   Security
1789 West Jefferson
Phoenix, AZ 85007
Tel: 602-542-2359

Arkansas
Office of Adoptions
Arkansas Department of Human
    Service
Division of Child and Family Service
P.O. Box 1437, Slot 808
Little Rock, AR 72203
Tel: 501-682-8462

California
Adoptions Branch
California Department of Social
    Services
744 P St. M/S 19-69
Sacramento, CA 95814
Tel: 916-445-3146

Colorado
Colorado Department of Social Services
1575 Sherman St., 2nd Floor
Denver, CO 80203
Tel: 303-866-3209

Connecticut
Connecticut Department of Children
    and Youth Services
Whitehall Building 2
Undercliff Rd.
Meriden, CT 06451
Tel: 203-238-6640

District of Columbia
District of Columbia Adoption
    and Placement Resources
Department of Human Services
609 H St., N.E., 3rd Floor
Washington, DC 20002
Tel: 202-724-8602

Delaware
Delaware Division of Child Protective
    Services
1825 Faulkland Rd.
Wilmington, DE 19805
Tel: 302-633-2638

Florida
Florida Department of Health
    & Rehabilitative Services
1317 Winewood Blvd.
Tallahassee, FL 32399
Tel: 904-487-2383

Georgia
Georgia Department of Human
    Resources
Division of Family and Child Services
2 Peachtree St. N.W., Ste. 414
Atlanta, GA 30303
Tel: 404-657-3560

Hawaii
Hawaii Department of Human Services
810 Richards St., Ste. 400
Honolulu, HI 96808
Tel: 808-586-5698

Idaho
Idaho Department of Health and Welfare
450 West State St., 3rd Floor
Boise, ID 83720-0036
Tel: 208-334-5700

Illinois
Illinois Department of Children
    and Family Services
100 West Randolph St., 6th Floor
Chicago, IL 60601
Tel: 217-524-2411

Indiana
Indiana Department of Public Welfare
402 West Washington St., W-364
Indianapolis, IN 46204
Tel: 888-204-7466

Iowa
Iowa Department of Human Services
Hoover State Office Building, 5th Floor
Des Moines, IA 50319
Tel: 515-281-5358

Kansas
Kansas Department of Social
  and Rehabilitative Services
300 SW Oakley St., West Hall
Topeka, KS 66606
Tel: 913-296-8138

Kentucky
Kentucky Cabinet for Human
  Resources
275 East Main St., 6th Floor
Frankfort, KY 40621
Tel: 502-564-2147

Louisiana
Louisiana Department of Social
  Services
333 Laurel St.
Baton Rouge, LA 70821
Tel: 504-342-2297

Maine
Maine Department of Human
  Services
221 State St.
Augusta, ME 04333
Tel: 207-287-5060

Maryland
Maryland Department of Human
  Resources, Social Services
311 West Saratoga St.
Baltimore, MD 21201
Tel: 410-767-7423

Massachusetts
Massachusetts Department of Social
  Services
24 Farnsworth St.
Boston, MA 02210
Tel: 617-727-0900

Michigan
Michigan Bureau of Family
  and Children Services

P.O. Box 30037
Lansing, MI 48909
Tel: 517-373-4021

Minnesota
Adoption Unit
Minnesota Department of Human
  Services
444 Lafayette, 1st Floor
St. Paul, MN 55155
Tel: 612-296-3740

Mississippi
Mississippi DHS/CFS
P.O. Box 352
Jackson, MS 39205
Tel: 601-359-4500

Missouri
Missouri Department of Social
  Services
Division of Family Services
P.O. Box 88
Jefferson City, MO 65103
Tel: 314-751-2502

Montana
Montana Department of Family
  Services
2300 12th Ave. S, Ste. 106
Helena, MT 59405
Tel: 406-444-5919

Nebraska
Nebraska Department of Social Services
P.O. Box 95026
Lincoln, NE 68509
Tel: 402-471-9331

Nevada
Office of Adoption
Nevada Children and Family Services
6171 W. Charleston Blvd., Bldg. 15
Las Vegas, NV 89158
Tel: 702-486-7650

New Hampshire
New Hampshire Division for Children
  and Youth Services
6 Hazen Dr.
Concord, NH 03301
Tel: 603-271-4707

New Jersey
New Jersey Division of Youth
  and Family Services
50 East State St., CN 717
Trenton, NJ 08625
Tel: 609-292-9139

New Mexico
New Mexico Human Services
  Department
P.O. Drawer 5160
Santa FE, NM 87502-5160
Tel: 505-827-8456

New York
New York State Department of Social
  Services
40 North Pearl St.
Albany, NY 12243
Tel: 518-474-2868

North Carolina
North Carolina Department of Human
  Resources
325 North Salisbury St.
Raleigh, NC 27603
Tel: 919-733-3801

North Dakota
North Dakota Department of Human
  Services
State Capitol
600 East Boulevard
Bismarck, ND 58505
Tel: 701-328-4805

Ohio
Division of Family Services
Ohio Department of Human Services

65 East State St., 5th Floor
Columbus, OH 43215
Tel: 614-466-9274

Oklahoma
Oklahoma Department of Human
  Services
P.O. Box 25352
Oklahoma City, OK 73125
Tel: 405-521-2475

Oregon
Oregon Department of Human Services
500 Summer St. NE, 2nd Floor
Salem, OR 97310
Tel: 503-945-5689

Pennsylvania
Pennsylvania Department of Public
  Welfare
Office of Children, Youth, and Families
P.O. Box 2675
Harrisburg, PA 17105
Tel: 717-787-7756

Rhode Island
Rhode Island Department of Children
  and Their Families
610 Mt. Pleasant, Building 5
Providence, RI 02908
Tel: 401-457-4548

South Carolina
South Carolina Department of Social
  Services
P.O. Box 1520
Columbia, SC 29202
Tel: 803-734-6095

South Dakota
South Dakota Department of Social
  Services
700 Governors Dr.
Pierre, SD 57501
Tel: 605-773-3227

Tennessee
Tennessee Department of Human
    Services
400 Deaderick St.
Nashville, TN 37248
Tel: 615-741-5935

Texas
Texas Department of Human Services
P.O. Box 149030 MC-W-415
Austin, TX 78714
Tel: 512-438-3412

Utah
Utah Division of Family Services
120 North 200 West, Rm. 225
Salt Lake City, UT 84103
Tel: 801-538-4080

Vermont
Vermont Division of Social Services
103 South Main St.
Waterbury, VT 05671
Tel: 802-241-2131

Virginia
Virginia Social Services
730 East Broad St., 2nd Floor
Richmond, VA 23219
Tel: 804-692-1273

Washington
Washington Division of Children
    and Family Services
Mail Stop 45710
Olympia, WA 98504
Tel: 360-902-7968

West Virginia
West Virginia Department of Human
    Services
Capitol Complex, Building 6, Rm. B850
Charleston, WV 25305
Tel: 304-558-7980

Wisconsin
Wisconsin Department of Health
    and Social Services
P.O. Box 7851
Madison, WI 53707
Tel: 608-266-3595

Wyoming
Wyoming Department of Health
    and Social Services
320 Hathaway Building
Cheyenne, WY 82002
Tel: 307-777-3570

RESOLVE Chapters (For infertile people seeking information and support)

Alabama
RESOLVE of Alabama
P.O. Box 360999-179
Birmingham, AL 35236
Tel: 205-969-8803

Alaska
RESOLVE of Alaska
P.O. Box 243234
Anchorage, AK 99524
Tel: 907-566-0022

Arizona
RESOLVE of Valley of the Sun
P.O. Box 54214
Phoenix, AZ 85078
Tel: 602-995-3933

Arkansas
RESOLVE of Northwest Arkansas
P.O. Box 4492
Fayetteville, AR 72702
Tel: 501-444-2186

California
Orange County RESOLVE, Inc.
P.O. Box 50693
Irvine, CA 92619-0693
Tel: 714-859-0580

RESOLVE of Greater Los Angeles
P.O. Box 15344
Los Angeles, CA 90015
Tel: 310-326-2630

RESOLVE of Northern
  California
312 Sutter St., 6th Floor
San Francisco, CA 94108
Business Office: 415-788-6772
Helpline: 415-788-3002

Colorado
RESOLVE of Colorado
P.O. Box 61096
Denver, CO 80206
Tel: 303-469-5261

Connecticut
RESOLVE of Fairfield County
P.O. Box 16763
Stamford, CT 06905-6763
Tel: 203-329-1147

RESOLVE of Greater Hartford
P.O. Box 370083
West Hartford, CT 06137-0083
Tel: 860-523-8337

District of Columbia
RESOLVE of Washington, DC,
  Metro Area, Inc.
P.O. Box 39221
Washington, DC 20016
Tel: 202-362-5555

Florida
RESOLVE of Fort Lauderdale
P.O. Box 16262

Fort Lauderdale, FL 33318
Tel: 954-749-9500

RESOLVE of the Palm Beaches
20423 State Rd. 7, Ste. 247
Boca Raton, FL 33498
Tel: 407-336-4420

Georgia
RESOLVE of Georgia
Box 343
2480-4 Briarcliff Rd.
Atlanta, GA 30329
Tel: 404-233-8443

Hawaii
RESOLVE of Hawaii
Bev Parker
P.O. Box 29193
Honolulu, HI 96280
Tel: 808-528-8559
  or 808-742-8885

Illinois
RESOLVE of Illinois
318 Half Day Rd., #300
Buffalo Grove, IL 60089-6547
Tel: 312-743-1623

Indiana
RESOLVE of Indiana
6103 Ashway Ct.
Indianapolis, IN 46205
Tel: 317-767-5999

Kansas
RESOLVE of Kansas City
P.O. Box 414603
Kansas City, MO 64141
Tel: 913-791-2432

Kentucky
RESOLVE of Kentucky
P.O. Box 22825
Lexington, KY 40522-2825

Louisiana
RESOLVE of Louisiana
P.O. Box 55693
Metairie, LA 70055-5693
Tel:504-454-6987

Maine
RESOLVE of Maine
P.O. Box 10691
Portland, ME 04104
Tel: 207-772-4783

Maryland
RESOLVE of Maryland
P.O. Box 5664
Baltimore, MD 21210
Tel: 410-243-0235

Massachusetts
RESOLVE of the Bay State
P.O. Box 1553
Waltham, MA 02254-1553
Tel: 617-647-1614

Michigan
RESOLVE of Michigan
P.O. Box 2185
Southfield, MI 48037
Tel: 810-680-0093
e-mail: KAE@mediaT.com

Minnesota
RESOLVE of Twin Cities
1021 Bandana Blvd. East,
    Ste. 228
St. Paul, MN 55108
Tel: 612-659-0333

Missouri
RESOLVE of St. Louis
P.O. Box 131
Hazelwood, MO 63042
Tel: 314-567-8788

Nebraska
RESOLVE of Nebraska

P.O. Box 24527
Omaha, NE 68124-0527
Tel: 402-449-6875

New Hampshire
RESOLVE of New Hampshire
12 Bayshore Dr.
Greenland, NH 03840-2204
Tel: 603-427-0410
(Meeting sites in Manchester, Dover,
    Derry, and Peterborough)

New Jersey
RESOLVE of New Jersey
P.O. Box 4335
Warren, NJ 07059-0335
Tel: 908-679-7171

New Mexico
RESOLVE of New Mexico
P.O. Box 13194
Albuquerque, NM 87192
Tel: 505-266-1170

Nevada
RESOLVE of Northern Nevada
P.O. Box 9749
Reno, NV 89507-9749
Tel: 702-852-3205

New York
RESOLVE of Capital District
P.O. Box 12901
Albany, NY 12212
Tel: 518-464-3848

RESOLVE of New York City
P.O. Box 185
Gracie Station, NY 10028
Tel: 212-764-0802 or
    718-507-4449 (Staten Island)

North Carolina
RESOLVE of Triangle, Inc.
P.O. Box 5564

Cary, NC 27511
Tel: 919-477-2360

Ohio
RESOLVE of Ohio
P.O. Box 770725
Lakewood, OH 44107
Tel: 1-800-414-OHIO

Oklahoma
RESOLVE of Oklahoma
4041 NW 33rd
Oklahoma City, OK 73112
Tel: 918-621-5250
    or 405-949-8857

Oregon
RESOLVE of Oregon
P.O. Box 40717
Portland, OR 97240
Tel: 503-762-0449

Pennsylvania
RESOLVE of Philadelphia
P.O. Box 0215
Merion Station, PA 19066-0215
Tel: 215-849-3920

RESOLVE of Pittsburgh
P.O. Box 11203
Pittsburgh, PA 15238-0203
Tel: 412-921-3501

RESOLVE of Southcentral PA
P.O. Box 402
Camp Hill, PA 17011
Tel: 717-234-8583

Rhode Island
RESOLVE of the Ocean State
P.O. Box 28201
Providence, RI 02908
Tel: 401-421-4695

South Carolina
RESOLVE of Upstate South Carolina

204 Fernbrook Circle
Spartanburg, SC 29307-2966

Tennessee
RESOLVE of Tennessee
4770 Germantown Rd., Ext., Ste. 327
Memphis, TN 38141
Tel: 901-541-5360

Texas
RESOLVE of Central Texas
P.O. Box 49783
Austin, TX 78765
Tel: 512-453-2171

RESOLVE of Dallas/Fort Worth
16831 Thomas Chapel Dr.
Grapewine, TX 75248
Tel: 214-250-9061

RESOLVE of Houston
P.O. Box 441212
Houston, TX 77244-1212
Tel: 713-975-5324

RESOLVE of South Texas
P.O. Box 782052
San Antonio, TX 78278
Tel: 210-967-6771

Utah
RESOLVE of Utah
P.O. Box 57531
Salt Lake City, UT 84157-0531
Tel: 801-483-4024

Vermont
RESOLVE of Vermont
P.O. Box 1094
Williston, VT 05495
Tel: 802-657-2542

Virginia
RESOLVE of Virginia
P.O. Box 70372
Richmond, VA 23255-0372
Tel: 804-751-5761 or 804-459-5856

Washington
RESOLVE of Washington State
P.O. Box 31231
Seattle, WA 98103-1231
Tel: 206-524-7257

Wisconsin
RESOLVE of Wisconsin
P.O. Box 13842
Wauwatosa, WI 53213-0842
Tel: 414-521-4590 or 608-231-9955

CANADA
Infertility Awareness Association
    of Canada
201-396 Cooper St.
Ottawa, Ontario
K2P 2H7 CANADA
Tel: 613-234-8585

Adoptive Parent Groups

Note: Telephone numbers are not
provided for all adoptive parent groups,
because some groups prefer to receive
only mail. E-mail addresses or FAX
numbers are included for some groups.
In some cases, contact names are also
included after the organization name.
This information is correct as of this
writing, but addresses do change.

Alabama
Alabama Friends of Adoption
Susan Markovitz, President of AFOA
P.O. Box 19025
Birmingham, AL 35219-9025
Tel: 205-290-0375

DeKalb County Families for Adoption
507 7th St. NW
Fort Payne, AL 35967

Parents Adopting Children Together
301 Deer Run Rd.
Auburn, AL 36830

Single Adoptive Parents Support
    Subgroup
2407 Titonka Rd.
Birmingham, AL 35244

Alaska
Anchorage Adoptive Parents
    Association
Fred Getty
550 W. Seventh Ave., Ste. 1320
Anchorage, AK 99501
Tel: 907-276-1680

Valley Adoptive Parents Association
P.O. Box 931
Palmer, AK 99645

Arizona
Advocates for Single Adoptive Parenting
    (A.S.A.P.)
Torin Scott, President
10105 E. Via Linda, #103-198
Scottsdale, AZ 85258
Tel: 602-951-8310 or 602-273-6055

Getting International Families
    Together
16053 N. 47th Dr.
Glendale, AZ 85306

Arkansas
Miracles
111 Devon Ct.
Jacksonville, AR 72076

River Valley Adoption Support Group
1005 W. 18th Terrace
Russellville, AR 72801-7025
Tel: 501-967-1641 (evenings)

California
Adoption Assistance & Support Group
16255 Ventura Blvd., Ste. 704
Encino, CA 91436-2312
Tel: 818-501-6800

Adoption Network
32392 Pacific Coast Highway
Loguna Beach, CA 92677-3300

FAIR
P.O. Box 51436
Palo Alto, CA 94303
Tel: 415-856-3513

For the Children
13074 Larkhaven Dr.
Moreno Valley, CA 92553-5689
Tel: 909-956-4240
e-mail: cking18178@aol.com

Hand in Hand
874 Phillip Ct.
Eldorado Hills, CA 95762

Intercountry Adoption Network (ICAN)
Karen Kirsein
9830 Canedo Ave.
Northridge, CA 91324
Tel: 818-772-8356

North Coast Adoptive Families
2136 Parrish Dr.
Santa Rosa, CA 95404-2323

Open Door Society of Los Angeles
12235 Silva Pl.
Cerritos, CA 90701

Orange County Adoptive Parent
    Association
39 Foxborn
Irvine, CA 92714-7524
Tel: 714-786-6494

Ours Through Adoption
Box 85152-343
San Diego, CA 92138

Patchwork Support Group
P.O. Box 5153
Stockton, CA 95205-0153

PACT
3904 Via Cardelina
Palos Verdes Estates, CA 90274

San Mateo Adoptive Parents
2136 Whipple Ave.
Redwood City, CA 94062

Single Adoptive Parents
385 S. 14th St.
San Jose, CA 95112

Single Adoptive Parents
1839 Catalina
Berkeley, CA 94707

Single Adoptive Parents of Los Angeles
Shelley Reben
7259 Balboa Blvd. #18
Van Nuys, CA 91406
Tel: 818-901-9519

Solano County Adoption Support Group
212 Sunhaven Dr.
Fairfield, CA 94533-5892

South Bay Adoption Support Group
Lil Snee, Executive Director
24662 Soquel-San Jose Rd.
Los Gatos, CA 95030-9226
Tel: 408-353-2995
FAX: 408-353-3166
e-mail: lilsnee@silverspoon.com

TEAM
1300 Astoria Pl.
Oxnard, CA 93030-8617

Colorado
Colorado Parents for All Children
780 E. Phillips Dr. S
Littleton, CO 80122
(Denver-Metro area)
(Publishes "How to Adopt in Colorado")

Colorado Parents for All Children
971 Burns Rd.
Colorado Springs, CO 80918

Connecticut
Adoptive Parents Exchange Group
6 Putnam Park Rd.
Bethel, CT 06801-2221

International Adoptive Families
433 Quarry Brook Dr.
South Windsor, CT 06074-3598

Latin America Parents Association
    of Connecticut, Inc.
P.O. Box 523
Unionville, CT 06085
(Parents who have adopted
or hope to adopt children
from Latin America)

Delaware
Adoptive Families with Information
    and Support (AFIS)
Mary Jo Wolfe
P.O. Box 7405
Wilmington, DE 19803
Helpline: 302-239-6232

District of Columbia
Association for Single Adoptive Parents
P.O. Box 1704
Springfield, VA 22151

Families for Private Adoption
P.O. Box 6375
Washington, DC 20015-0375

North Virginia FACE
103 15th St., N.E.
Washington, DC 20002-6505

Florida
The Lifeline for Children
P.O. Box 17184
Plantation, FL 33318
Tel: 954-979-1314

PACE
P.O. Box 560293

Rockledge, FL 32956
Tel: 407-639-8895

Parents Adoption Lifeline
536 Inlet Rd.
North Palm Beach, FL 33048
Tel: 561-433-8200

Single Adoption Parent Support
    Group
Cherokee Pilots Association
504 El Sereno Pl #152
Tampa, FL 33603

Special Needs Adoption Support Group
    (SNAP)
15913 Layton Ct.
Tampa, FL 33647
Tel: 813-978-8183

Georgia
Adopted Kids & Parents
4137 Bellflower Ct.
Roswell, GA 30075

Adopt Parents Association
318 Suncrest Blvd.
Savannah, GA 31410

Augusta Adoption League
P.O. Box 15353
Augusta, GA 30919

Clarke County Adoption Resource
    Exchange
Box 6311
Athens, GA 30604-6311

Georgia Adoptive Parents
1722 Wilmont Dr. NE
Atlanta, GA 30329

Georgia Council on Adoptable Children
3559 London Rd.
Chamblee, GA 30341-2041

Hawaii
Adoptive Families of Kauai

1702 Makoi St.
Lihue, HI 96766
Tel: 808-246-0844

Forever Families
Adoption Support and Newsletter
Peggy Kuharcik
7719 Waikapu Loop
Honolulu, HI 96825
Tel: 808-396-9130
e-mail: Foreverfam@aol.com

Idaho
Adopt Families of SE Idaho
2356 Oak Trail Dr.
Idaho Falls, ID 83404

Families Involved in Adoption
P.O. Box 612
Priest River, ID 83856-0612

Illinois
Adoptive Families Today
P.O. Box 1726
Barrington, IL 60011-1726
Tel: 847-382-0858

All-Dopt
Marietta Bear
727 Ramona Pl.
Godfrey, IL 62035
Tel: 618-466-8926
(Mostly international but also U.S.)

Central Illinois Adoptive Families
2206 Oakwood Ave.
Bloomington, IL 61704-2414
Tel: 309-662-3349

Chicago Area Families for Adoption
1212 S. Naper Blvd., Ste. 119
Naperville, IL 60540

Child International
4121 Crestwood Dr.
Northbrook, IL 60062-7544

Tel: 847-272-2511
FAX: 847-509-9740
(Most members live in Chicago
and northern suburbs.)

Christian Adoption Ministries
327 N. High
Carlinville, IL 62626

DeKalb Area Adoptive Families
Mary Kowalski
303 N. 2nd St.
De Kalb, IL 60115-3236
Tel: 815-758-4307 or
Kathy McGinnis-Craft 815-758-2355
e-mail: HeronCover@aol.com

Fox Valley Adoption Support Group
1111 Adobe Dr.
Aurora, IL 60506-1603

Hands Around the World
1417 E. Miner St.
Arlington Heights, IL 60004

Illiana Adoptive Parents
P.O. Box 412
Flossmoor, IL 60422

Illinois Council on Adoptable
  Children
8302 McCormick Blvd.
Skokie, IL 60076

Ours of Northern Illinois
12510 Thistle Ridge Ct.
Roscoe, IL 61073

SCIAPA
39 Meander Pike
Chatham, IL 62629

Stars of David International, Inc.
Susan M. Katz, Director
3175 Commercial Ave., Ste. 100
Northbrook, IL 60062-1915
Tel: 800-STAR-349

Transracial Adoptive Moms
121 E. Robinhood Way
Bolingbrook, IL 60440

Uniting Families Foundation
95 W. Grand Ave., Ste. 206
Lake Villa, IL 60046
Tel: 847-356-1452

Indiana
Adoptive Family Network
306 Sharon Rd.
W. Lafayette, IN 47906

Families Adopt Children Together
52041 Sherfort Ct.
Granger, IN 46530

OURS Through Adoption
RR 3 104 S. Water St.
Monroeville, IN 46773-9301
Tel: 219-623-3166
(Mostly international adoption,
but all welcome)

Iowa
Adoptive Families of Greater
  Des Moines
1690 Northwest Dr.
Des Moines, IA 50310

Cedar Valley Adoption Group
118 N. Eighth St.
Osage, IA 50461

Central Iowa Adoptive Families
3740 Blanshan Dr.
Ames, IA 50010

Iowa Foster & Adoptive Parents
100 Court Ave.
Des Moines, IA 50309

Iowa City International Adoptive
  Families
1328 Melrose Ave.
Iowa City, IA 52246-1726

Iowans for International Adoption
31496 Iron Bridge Rd.
Spragueville, IA 52074-9758

Kansas
International Families of Mid-America
6708 Granada Rd.
Prairie Village, KS 66208

Parents by Choice
6100 W. 58th St.
Mission, KS 66202

Kentucky
Adoptive Parents Guild
1888 Douglas Rd.
Louisville, KY 40205

Families & Adoptive Children Together
150 Ridgemont Rd.
Paducah, KY 42003
Tel: 502-554-0203

OK Kids
7406 Vincent Way
Louisville, KY 40214-3851
(Focus on children adopted from Korea
and their families)

PACK, Inc.
139 Highland Dr.
Madisonville, KY 42431-9154
Tel: 502-825-2158
(International adoption, mostly from
Korea and China)

Louisiana
Adopt Older Kids, Inc. (A-OK)
818 Briarwood Dr.
New Iberia, LA 70560

Adoptive Couples Together
P.O. Box 1311
Kenner LA 70063

Korean-American Resource
  Exchange
4107 St. Elizabeth Dr.
Kenner, LA 70065

Maine

Adoptive Families of Maine
17 Pike St.
Augusta, ME 04330

Adoptive Families of Maine
129 Sunderland Dr.
Auburn, ME 04210

Maryland

Adoptive Families and Friends
Monique Secula
1440 Hunting Horn Lane
Frederick, MD 21703
Tel: 301-695-2574

Adoptive Family Network
P.O. Box 7
Columbia, MD 21045
Tel: 410-553-0889
   or 301-984-6133
(Education, support and advocacy;
pre-adoption classes)

Center for Adoptive Families
10230 New Hampshire Ave,
   Ste. 200
Silver Spring, MD 20903
Tel: 301-493-2900
e-mail: adopt@aol.com
(Support programs, counseling
and education, annual conference
of entire adoption community)

Children in Common
Janice Pearse
3335 Governor Martin Ct.
Ellicott City, MD 21043
Tel: 410-203-9613

FACE
P.O. Box 28058
Northwood Station
Baltimore, MD 21239

Latin American Parents Association
Sydney Jacobs

Box 4403
Silver Spring, MD 20914-4403

Rainbow Families
Jim and Terri Cooney
128 E. Lynbrook Pl.
Bel Air, MD 21014-5415
Tel: 410-838-3858
(Families formed by domestic,
transracial adoption, black or racially
mixed children; resource for couples
seeking to adopt)

Massachusetts

Latin American Adoptive Families
23 Evangeline Rd.
Falmouth, MA 02540

Merrimac Valley Open Door
   Society
36 Orchard St.
Merrimac, MA 01860-1812

North Shore Open Door Society
16 Harrison Ave.
Gloucester, MA 01930-1804

Open Door Society of MA
Joan Clark
1750 Washington St.
Holliston, MA 01746-2234
Tel: 1-800-93ADOPT (in-state)
FAX: 508-429-2261

Single Parents Adopting Children
   Everywhere (SPACE)
6 Sunshine Ave.
Natick, MA 01760

Michigan

Adopt
6939 Shields Ct.
Saginaw, MI 48609

Bethany Christian Service Adoptive
   Parent Forum
901 Eastern Ave NE
Grand Rapids, MI 49503

European Adoptive Families
of MI
P.O. Box 87894
Canton, MI 48187-4826
Tel: 313-981-6534

Families for International Children
6475 28th St. SE #124
Grand Rapids, MI 49546

Families of Latin Kids (FOLK)
Kathi Nelson
Box 15537
Ann Arbor, MI 48108

The Family Tree Support Group
27821 Santa Barbara Dr.
Lathrup Village, MI 48076-3355
Tel: 248-557-3501

Greater Lansing Ours
by Adoption
Box 25161
Lansing, MI 48909-5161

Latin American Families Through
Adoption (LAFTA)
Sabina Seidel
608 Marcelletti Ave.
Paw Paw, MI 49079-1219
Tel: 616-657-6498

Michigan Association of Single
Adoptive Parents (MASAP)
7412 Coolidge Ave.
Center Line, MI 48015-2049
Tel: 810-758-6909

PACE
P.O. Box 8423
Holland, MI 49422-8423

West Michigan Friends
of Adoption
7635 Yorktown St.
Richland, MI 49083
Tel: 616-629-9037

Minnesota
Families of Multi Racial Adoptions
2057 Roe Crest Dr.
Mankato, MN 56003-3434

Families Supporting Adoption
11462 Crow Hassan Park Rd.
Hanover, MN 55341-9404

Niños del Paraguay
7801 Bush Lake Dr.
Bloomington, MN 55438-3201

Northland Families Through
Adoption
518 Lagarde Rd.
Wrenswall, MN 55797

Rochester Area Adoptive Families
Together (RAAFT)
729 Ninth St. SW
Rochester, MN 55902

Missouri
Adoption Today
Mary Kay Helldoerfer
5350 Casa Royale Dr.
St. Louis, MO 63129-3007
Tel: 314-894-4586

Families Through Adoption
1350 Summit Dr.
Fenton, MO 63026

Single Mothers By Choice
4320 Genessee
Kansas City, MO 64111

Montana
Adoptive Families of Montana
1499 Cobb Hill Rd.
Bozeman, MT 59715

FACET
930 Ave. B NW
Great Falls, MT 59401

Families for Adoptable Children
P.O. Box 485
Anaconda, MT 59711

Yellowstone International Families
5028 Rimrock Rd.
Billings, MT 59106

Nebraska
Families Through Adoption
Lori Erickson
1619 Coventry Lane
Grand Island, NE 68801-7025
Tel: 308-381-8743

Open Hearts Adoption Support Group
4023 S. 81st St.
Lincoln, NE 68506

Nevada
Southern Nevada Adoption Association
1316 Saylor Way
Las Vegas, NV 89108
Tel: 702-647-0201

New Hampshire
Open Door Society of New Hampshire
P.O. Box 792
Derry, NH 03038
Tel: 603-437-0426

New Jersey
Adoptive Single Parents
  of New Jersey
107 Maple St.
Haworth, NJ 07641

Camden County FACES
130 Mansfield Blvd. S
Cherry Hill, NJ 08034-3615

Concerned Persons for Adoption
P.O. Box 179
Whippany, NJ 07981
Tel: 908-273-5694

Links
91 Carlton Ave.
Washington, NJ 07882

Rainbow Families
670 Oakley Pl.
Oradell, NJ 07649

Today's Adoptive Families
30 Manchester Way
Burlington, NJ 08016
Tel: 609-386-7237

New Mexico
Parents of Inter Cultural
  Adoptions
P.O. Box 91175
Albuquerque, NM 87199

New York
Adoptive Parents Committee Hudson
  Region Chapter
P.O. Box 245
White Plains, NY 10605-0245
Tel: 914-997-7859

Adoptive Parents Committee
P.O. Box 3525
Church St. Station
New York, NY 10008-3525
Tel: 212-304-8479

Adoptive Parents Committee
Long Island Chapter
P.O. Box 71
Bellmore, NY 11710

Champlain Valley Adoption Fam.
44 Sally Ave.
Plattsburgh, NY 12901-1729

Council of Adoptive Parents
  (COAP)
P.O. Box 964
Penfield, NY 14526
Tel: 716-383-0947

FAX: 716-387-9841
e-mail: tlsavina@naz.edu

GIFT
143 W. 4th St.
New York, NY 10024

New York Singles Adopting Children
    (NYSAC)
Barbara Stern
P.O. Box 472
Glen Oaks, NY 11004
Tel: 212-254-1696

Richmond Adoptive Parents, Inc.
P.O. Box 020665
Staten Island, NY 10302

Southern Tier Adoptive Families
3617 Lome Dr.
Endwell, NY 13760
Tel: 607-748-4172

Upstate New York Single Adoptive
    Parents
38 Shaker Dr. Blvd.
Londonville, NY 12211
Florence Abrams: 518-489-4322
Kathy McGee: 518-581-0891
(Call in evenings; long distance
calls will not be returned unless
they can be made collect.)

Western New York Single Parents
    for Adoption
73 Cleveland Dr.
Kenmore, NY 14223

North Carolina
Adoptive Families Heart
    to Heart
456 NC Highway 62 East
Greensboro, NC 27406
Tel: 910-674-5024
(Special interest in adopted children
over age two)

Capital Area Families for Adoption
108 North Drawbridge Lane
Cary, NC 27513

Carolina Adoptive Families
1005 Black Oak Dr.
Matthews, NC 28105-5501

Coastal Hearts of Adoption
Debbie Lilley
6002 McLean St.
Emerald Isle, NC 28594
Tel: 919-354-5826

Stars of David
Wake County Jewish Federation
12804 Norwood Rd.
Raleigh, NC 27613
Tel: 919-676-6170

Tri-Adopt
P.O. Box 51192
Shannon Plaza
Durham, NC 27717

North Dakota
Adoption in Our Heart
2578 Willow Rd. NE
Fargo, ND 58102

Families & Friends of Adoption
1814 Lewis Blvd.
Grand Forks, ND 58201

Ohio
Adoptive Families Support Association
John Seavers
P.O. Box 91247
Cleveland, OH 44101
Tel: 216-491-4638
(Support group, introductory sessions,
annual culture camp, social activities, etc.)

Adoptive Families of Greater Cincinnati
4 Revel Ct.
Cincinnati, OH 45217-1916

Group of Adoptive Black Parents
Robert Simpson
1055 Grayview Ct.
Cincinnati, OH 45224
Tel: 513-541-4166

New Roots Adoption Support Group
Stacey Moore
P.O. Box 14953
Columbus, OH 43214
Tel: 614-470-0846

Rainbow Families of Toledo
Nancy Shanks
1920 S. Shore Blvd.
Oregon, OH 43618
Tel: 419-693-9259

Southeast Ohio Adoptive Family
  Support Group
MaryAnn Linscott
P.O. Box 75
Athens, OH 45701
(Monthly meetings)

Oklahoma
Adoptive Families Support Association
  (AFSA)
c/o Judy Smith
1301 Charlton Rd.
Edmond, OK 73003
Tel: 405-359-0812

Adopt a Special Kid (AASK),
  OK Chapter
c/o Adoption Support
P.O. Box 25
Harrah, OK 73045
FAX: 405-454-1179
(All-volunteer group)

Oregon
Adoptive Families Unlimited
Lynn Stevens

Box 40752
Eugene, OR 97404
Tel: 541-688-1654
e-mail: adoptfam@juno.com

Northwest Adoptive Families
  Association
P.O. Box 25355
Portland, OR 97225-0355

Rogue Valley Adoptive Families
1156 Conestoga St.
Grants Pass, OR 97527-5381

Pennsylvania
Adoptive Families with Information and
  Support
RR#1, Box 23
Landerburg, PA 19350

Concerned Adoptive Parents
701 Country Club Rd.
Warrington, PA 18976

Families Through Adoption
4109 Kingswood Ct.
Harrisburg, PA 17112

Families Together
Apollo Lane
Rochester, PA 15074

International Adoptive Families
402 Pebblecreek Dr.
Cranberry Township, PA 16066-5652

Single Adoptive Parents of Delaware
  Valley
1415 Arline Ave.
Roslyn, PA 19001

South Carolina
Piedmont Adoptive Families
Box 754
Spartanburg, SC 29304-0754
Tel: 864-578-3571

South Dakota

Adoptive Families of Black Hills
3701 Reder St.
Rapid City, SD 57702-2242

Families Through Adoption
Box 851
Sioux Falls, SD 57101

Tennessee

Mid-South Families Through Adoption
6151 Ashley Rd.
Arlington, TN 38002

Ours of Middle Tennessee
Wanda Beck
3557 Bethlehem Rd.
Springfield, TN 37172
Tel: 615-643-3426
e-mail: 74532.3114@compuserve.com

Texas

Adopting Children Together
P.O. Box 120966
Arlington, TX 76012
Tel: 817-467-4778

Adoptive Families Together
Box 272963
Houston, TX 77277-2963

Austin Kids From All Cultures
Ron and Pam Matthews
4508 Sinclair
Austin, TX 78756

Council on Adoptable Children—Dallas
P.O. Box 141199
Dallas, TX 75214-1199

Interracial Family Alliance of Houston
P.O. Box 16248
Houston, TX 77222
Tel: 281-586-8949

North Texas Families for Adoption
Box 29903
Dallas, TX 75229

Romanian Cousins
Cheryl Long
382 Bedford Dr.
Richardson, TX 75080
Tel: 972-644-7921

Vermont

The Chosen Children from Romania
P.O. Box 401
Barre, VT 05641-0401
Tel: 802-479-2848
FAX: 802-476-3445

Vermont Families Through Adoption
16 Aspen Dr.
Essex Junction, VT 05452

Virginia

Adoption Resource Exchange for Single
  Parents
P.O. Box 5782
Springfield, VA 22150-9998

Adoptive Families Hand in Hand
P.O. Box 1175
Culpeper, VA 22701

Association of Single Adoptive Parents
P.O. Box 3618
Merrifield, VA 22116-3618
Tel: 804-798-2673

Blue Ridge Adoption Group
c/o Commonwealth Catholic Charities
820 Campbell Ave. SW
Roanoke, VA 24016

Families for Russian & Ukrainian
  Adoptions
Box 2944
Merrifield, VA 22116-2944
Tel: 703-560-6184

People for the Adoption of Children
8305 Bronwood Rd.
Richmond, VA 23229

Romanian Children's Connection
1206 Hillside Terrace
Alexandria, VA 22302

Washington
Adoptive Families Network
  of S. Puget Sound
Box 112188
Tacoma, WA 98411-2188

Adoptive Families United
1537 NE 92nd St.
Seattle, WA 98115
Tel: 206-527-0425

Advocates for Single Adoptive Parents,
  NW
5706 NE 204th St.
Seattle, WA 98155

Families With Children From China
c/o Corpserve, Inc.
1001 Fourth Ave., Ste. 4500
Seattle, WA 98154
Tel: 206-323-0886

KIN/OURS Adoptive Family Group
P.O. Box 5459
Everett, WA 98206

Kitsap Adoption Group
Marilyn Wistrand
5219 NE Falcon Ridge Lane
Poulsboro, WA 98370
Tel: 360-697-2997

Supporting Special Families
  with Encouragement
  (SSAFE)
5581 2nd Ave.

Ferndale, WA 98248
Tel: 360-671-6516

West Virginia
AFFA
Box 2775
Charleston, WV 25330-2775

Wisconsin
Adoptive Families of Greater
  Milwaukee, Inc.
Aggie Hale
15385 Glenora Ct.
New Berlin, WI 53151
Tel: 414-860-0940

Adoptive Parent Group of Southern
  Wisconsin
1408 Vilas Ave.
Madison, WI 53711
Tel: 608-251-0736

Lakeshore Adoptive Families
1616 Jasmine Dr.
Manitowoc, WI 54220-2224
Tel: 414-683-1843
e-mail: bjbrul@dataplusnet.com

U.S./Chilean Adoptive Families
  (USCAF)
J. Morack
2041 N 107th
Milwaukee, WI 53226-2329
Tel: 414-257-0248

Wisconsin Association of Single
  Adoptive Parents
Laurie Glass
4520 N. Bartlett Ave.
Shorewood, WI 53211-1509
Tel: 414-962-9342

Wisconsin Single Parents
810 Richards St.
Watertown, WI 53094

Wyoming
Northern Wyoming Adoptive
  Parents
Box 788
Basin, WY 82410

CANADA
Adoptive Parents Association
  of Alberta
Carol Morton
Box 6496
Bonnyville, Alberta
Canada T9N 2H1

Adoptive Parents Association
  of BC
Box 8600, Ste. 16
Revelstoke, BC
Canada V0E 2S0

Adoptive Parents Association
  of British Columbia
#205-15463 104 ve.
Surrey, BC
Canada V3R 1N9

SAPA
210-2002 Quebec Ave.
Saskatoon, SASK
Canada S7K 1W4

St. John Adoptive Parents
  Association
236 McNamara Dr.
St. John, NB
Canada E2J 3L4

Society of Special Needs Adoptive
  Parents
1150 409 Granville St.
Vancouver, BC
Canada V6C 1T2

Selected Internet Listings

(The ones listed here are just a sampling!)

Adoption Oklahoma
http://www.boonesmith.com/adoptok/

Adoptive Families of America
http://www.adoptivefam.org/2-0/2-0.html

Bethany Adoption Services
http://www.ihr.com/infertility/adoption.
  html

Children Awaiting Placement (CAP)
http://www.adopt.org/adopt/cap/cap.html

Families of Russian and Ukrainian
  Adoption (FRUA)
http://www.serve.com/fredt/adopt.html

General Adoption Information
http://www.adopting.com/agencies.html

Indiana Adoption Resource Center
http://www.state.in.us/fssa/adoption/

Massachusetts Department of Social
  Services
http://www.DSS-Info@state.ma.us

Michigan Adoption Resource Exchange
http:www.mare.org/Start.html

National Adoption Center
http://www.adopt.org/adopt/adoptqst.html

National Adoption Information
  Clearinghouse
http://www.calib.com/naic/index.htm
(Established by Congress to
provide information to the
general public on many aspects
of adoption)

National Council For Adoption
http://www.NCFA-us.org

New York Department of Social
  Services
http://www.state.ny.us/dss/adopt

North American Council on Adoptable
  Children
http://www.openadoption.org/nacac.htm

RESOLVE
http://www.resolve.org/

Tapestry Books
http://www.webcom.com/tapestry/
(Provides a catalog of most adoption
books in print)

Texas Adoption Resource Exchange
http://www.tdprs.state.tx.us/adoption/tare
  .html

Wendy's (Adopting a Child with Special
  Needs)
http://www.wendys.com/wendys/htm

BIBLIOGRAPHY

Adamec, Christine and Pierce, William L. *The Encyclopedia of Adoption* (New York: Facts on File, 1991).

Adamec, Christine. "Kids Aren't Perfect, Even If They're Born as 'Healthy Infants,' " in *Report on Intercountry Adoption 1997* (Boulder, Colorado: International Concerns for Children).

Adamec, Christine. *There ARE Babies to Adopt: A Resource Guide for Prospective Parents* (New York: Kensington Books, 1996).

Alexander-Roberts, Colleen. *The Legal Adoption Guide: Safely Navigating the System* (Dallas: Taylor Publishing, 1996).

Ambert, Anne-Marie. *The Effect of Children on Parents* (New York: The Haworth Press, 1992).

"At Risk For Psychosis." *Harvard Mental Health Letter* 12 (April 1996): 7.

Belsky, Jay, and Kelly, John. *The Transition to Parenthood: How a First Child Changes a Marriage, Why Some Couples Grow Closer and Others Apart* (New York: Dell, 1994).

Benson, Peter L., Sharma, Anu R., and Roehlkepartain, Eugene C. *Growing Up Adopted: A Portrait of Adolescents and Their Families* (Minneapolis: The Search Institute, 1994).

Berrick, Jill Duerr, and Lawrence-Karski, Ruth. "Emerging Issues in Child Welfare." *Public Welfare* 53 (Fall 1995): v. 4(8).

Billings, J. R. "Bonding Theory—Tying Mothers In Knots? A Critical Review of the Application of a Theory to Nursing." *Journal of Clinical Nursing* 4 (July 1995) 207–211.

Blanton, Terril L., and Deschner, Jeanne. "Biological Mothers' Grief: The Postadoptive Experience in Open Versus Confidential Adoption." *Child Welfare* LXIX (November/December 1990): 525–535.

Boer, Fritz, et al., "International Adoption of Children with Siblings: Behavioral Outcomes," *American Journal of Orthopsychiatry* 64 (April 1994): 252–262.

Bohman, Michael. *Adopted Children and Their Families* (Stockholm: Proprius, 1970).

Bowlby, John. *Maternal Care and Mental Health* (Geneva: World Health Organization, 1951).

Cadoret, Remi J. "Adoption Studies." *Alcohol, Health & Research World* 19 (Summer 1995): 195(6).

Cadoret, R. J., et al., "Adoption Study Demonstrating Two Genetic Pathways to Drug Abuse." *Archives of General Psychiatry* 52 (January 1995): 42–52.

Chess, Stella, and Thomas, Alexander. *Temperament: Theory and Practice* (New York: Brunner/Mazel, 1996).

Chippindale-Bakker, Victoria, and Foster, Linda. "Adoption in the 1990s: Sociodemographic Determinants of Biological Parents Choosing Adoption." *Child Welfare* 75 (July 1, 1996): 337.

Cowan, Carolyn Pape, and Cowan, Philip A. "Is There Love After Baby?" *Psychology Today* 25 (July–August 1992): 58(8).

Crouch, M., and Manderson, L. "The Social Life of Bonding Theory." *Social Science Medicine* 41 (Sept. 1995): 837–844.

Custer, Marcia. "Adoption as an Option for Unmarried Teens." *Adolescence* 28 (Winter 1993): 891(12).

Daniels, Ken R. "Adoption and Donor Insemination: Factors Influencing Couples' Choices." *Child Welfare* LXXIII (January–February 1994): 5–14.

DiGiulio, J. F. "Self-Acceptance: A Factor in the Adoption Process." *Child Welfare* 67 (Sept.–Oct. 1988): 423–429.

Edelstein, Susan B. *Children with Prenatal and/or Other Drug Exposure: Weighing the Risks of Adoption* (Washington, D.C.: The Child Welfare League of America, 1995).

Eiden, R. D., Teti, D. M., and Corns, K. M. "Maternal Working Models of Attachment, Marital Adjustment, and the Parent-Child Relationship." *Child Development* 66 (October 1995): 1504–1518.

Erichsen, Heino. "From the Desk of Heino Erichsen: The Current International Adoption Situation." *News of Los Niños,* November–December 1996, 8.

Eyer, Diane E. *Mother-Infant Bonding: A Scientific Fiction* (New Haven, Conn.: Yale University Press, 1992).

Falciglia, Grace A., and Norton, Philippa A. "Evidence for a Genetic Influence on Preference for Some Foods." *Journal of the American Dietetic Association* 94 (Feb. 1994): 154(5).

"Family ties: Desire Outweighs DNA," *Science News*, 27 May 1995, 333.

Fergusson, David M., Lynskey, Michael, and Horwood, L. John. "The Adolescent Outcomes of Adoption: A 16-Year Longitudinal Study." *Journal of Child Psychology and Psychiatry* 36, no. 4 (1995): 597–615.

Field, Tiffany. "Attachment and Separation in Young Children." *Annual Review of Psychology* 47 (1996): 541–561.

Ge, Ziaojia, et al. "The Developmental Interface Between Nature and Nurture: A Mutual Influence Model of Child Antisocial Behavior and Parent Behaviors." *Developmental Psychology* 32 no. 4 (1996): 574–589.

Gerbner, George B. *Adoption in the Mass Media: A Preliminary Survey of Sources of Information and a Pilot Study*. Unpublished report. The Annenberg School of Communications, University of Pennsylvania, Philadelphia, November 21, 1988.

Gleick, Elizabeth. "Rumor and Rage." *People Weekly*, April 25, 1994, 78(3).

Golombok, Susan, Cook, Rachel, and Bish, Alison. "Families Created by the New Reproductive Technologies: Quality of Parenting and Social and Emotional Development of the Children." *Child Development* 66, no. 2 (1995): 285–298.

Groze, Vic. "Adoption and Single Parents: A Review." *Child Welfare* LXX (May/June 1991): 321–332.

Halfon, Neal, et al. "Health Status of Children in Foster Care: The Experience of the Center for the Vulnerable Child." *Archives of Pediatrics & Adolescent Medicine* 149 (April 1995): 386(7).

Hirsch, Anne M., and Hirsch, Stephen, M. "The Long-Term Psychosocial Effects of Infertility." *Journal of Obstetric, Gynecologic and Neonatal Nursing* 24, no. 6 (1995): 517–522.

Holden, Constance. "Small Refugees Suffer the Effects of Early Neglect." *Science* 274, 15 November 1996, 1076(2).

Hostetter, Margaret K., and Johnson, Dana. "Medical Examination of the Internationally Adopted Child." *Postgraduate Medicine* 99 (April 1991): 70(7).

Hotline Information Packet. National Council For Adoption, Washington, D.C., 1996.

Jenista, Jerri Ann. "Creating a Support Network." *Adoptive Families*, September/October 1994, 34–35.

Jenista, Jerri Ann. "Medical Primer for the Adoptive Parents." In *Handbook for Single Adoptive Parents*, ed. Hope Marindin (Chevy Chase, MD.: National Council of Single Adoptive Parents, 1997).

Jenista, Jerri Ann. "Schizophrenia: The Cancer of Psychiatry." *Adoption/Medical News* 3 (January 1997).

Jewett, Claudia L. *Adopting the Older Child* (Boston: Harvard Common Press, 1978).

Jirka, J., Schuett, S., and Foxall, M. J. "Loneliness and Social Support in Infertile Couples." *Journal of Obstetrical Gynecology Neonatal Nursing* 25 (Jan. 1996): 55–60.

Kim, Wun Jung. "International Adoption: A Case Review of Korean Children." *Child Psychiatry and Human Development* 25 (Spring 1995): 141–154.

Levy-Shiff, Rachel, Goldshmidt, Ilana, and Har-Even, Dov. "Transition to Parenthood in Adoptive Families." *Developmental Psychology* 27, no. 1 (1991): 131–140.

Lopez, Charlotte, with Dworkin, Susan. *Lost in the System* (New York: Fireside, 1996).

McKay, Matthew, Davis, Martha, and Fanning, Patrick. *Messages: The Communication Book* (Oakland, CA: New Harbinger Publications, 1995).

Medoff, Marshall H. "An Empirical Analysis of Adoption." *Economic Inquiry* 31 (Jan. 1993): 59(12).

Meyerhoff, Michael K. "The Bonding Period." *Pediatrics for Parents*, December 1992, 6(3).

Miall, Charlene E. "The Stigma of Adoptive Parent Status: Perceptions of Community Attitudes Toward Adoption and the Experience of Informal Social Sanctioning." *Family Relations* 36, January 1987, 34–39.

Miller, Laurie, et al. "Developmental and Nutritional Status of Internationally Adopted Children." *Archives of Pediatrics & Adolescent Medicine* 149 (Jan. 1995): 40(5).

National Council For Adoption. *The Adoption Factbook* (Washington, D.C., 1989).

Nulman, Irena, et al. "Neurodevelopment of Adopted Children Exposed in Utero to Cocaine." *Canadian Medical Association Journal* 151, no. 4 (1994): 1591–1597.

Nulman, Irena, et al. "Neurodevelopment of Children Exposed in Utero to Antidepressant Drugs." *The New England Journal of Medicine* 336 (January 23, 1997): 258–262.

Parens, Erik. "Taking Behavioral Genetics Seriously." *The Hastings Center Report* 26 (July–August 1996): 13(6).

Phipps, Su Ann Arnn. "A Phenomenological Study of Couples' Infertility: Gender Influence." In *Qualitative Research in Nursing: Advancing the Humanistic Imperative* (Philadelphia: Lippincott, 1995).

Pilowsky, D. "Psychopathology Among Children Placed in Family Foster Care." *Psychiatric Services* 46 (September 1995): 906–910.

Post, Stephen G. "Adoption and the Culture of Obstetrics." *America* 174, 23 March 1996, 16(4).

"So Long, Superparents." *Psychology Today*, May–June 1993, 16.

Rafuse, Jill. "Growing Number of Overseas Adoptions Leads to Recommendations from Manitoba M.D.s." *Canadian Medical Association Journal* 152 (May 15, 1995): 1669–1670.

Reinke, Peter S. "Interracial Adoption Studies Show Environment Influences Achievement." *The Brown University Child and Adolescent Behavior Letter* 9 (Dec. 1993): 1(2).

"Rethinking the Decision to Have Children: When, How and Whether or Not to Bear Children." *American Behavioral Scientist* 37, (August 1994): 1058(16).

Rutter, Michael. "Romanian Orphans Adopted Early Overcome Deprivation." *The Brown University Child and Adolescent Behavior Letter* 12 (June 1996): 1(3).

Rutter, Virginia. "Who Stole Fertility?" *Psychology Today*, March–April 1996, 49(9).

Salzer, Linda P. *Surviving Infertility: A Compassionate Guide Through the Emotional Crisis of Infertility* (New York: HarperCollins, 1991).

Sandelowski, Margarete. "A Theory of the Transition to Parenthood of Infertile Couples." *Research in Nursing & Health* 18 (April 1995): 123–132.

Schmitz, S., et al. "Genetic and Environmental Influences on Temperament in Middle Childhood: Analyses of Teacher and Tester Ratings." *Child Development* 67 (Apr. 1996): 409–422.

Schwartz, Lita Linzer. "Biological and Non-Biological Families Face the Same Challenges." *The Brown University Child and Adolescent Behavior Letter* 11 (Jan. 1995): 8.

Sherrod, R. A., "A Male Perspective on Infertility." *Maternal Care Nursing* 20 (Sept.–Oct. 1995): 269–275.

Simeon, Jovan G., Wiggins, Doreen M., and Williams, Esther. "Worldwide Use of Psychotropic Drugs in Child and Adolescent Psychiatric Disorders." *Progress in Neuro-Psychopharmacology & Biological Psychiatry* 19 (1995): 455–465.

Simon, Harriet Fishman. *Wanting Another Child: Coping with Secondary Infertility* (New York: Lexington Books, 1995).

Simon, Rither, and Thompson, Alice G. "Should White Families Be Allowed to Adopt African American Children?" *Health* 7, July–August 1993, 22.

"Six-Week Examination After Delivery or Adoption," *American Family Physician* 43 (June 1991): 2252.

Smith, Dorothy W., and Sherwen, Laurie Nehls. *Mothers and Their Adopted Children: The Bonding Process* (New York: Tiresias Press, 1983).

Smith, Jerome, and Miroff, Franklin I. *You're Our Child: The Adoption Experience* (Lanham, Md.: Madison Books, 1987).

Snarey, John. "Men Without Children: Husbands Cope With Infertility in Different Ways." *Psychology Today* 22, March 1988, 61(2).

Terwogt, Mark Meerum, et al. "Common Beliefs About the Heredity of Human Characteristics." *British Journal of Psychology* 84 (Nov. 1993): 499(5).

Thomas, Irene Middleman. "Yours, Mine, and Whose?" *Hispanic* 6 (Dec. 1993): 26(4).

Verhulst, F. C., and Bieman, Versluis-den. "Developmental Course of Problem Behaviors in Adolescent Adoptees." *Journal of American Academy of Child & Adolescent Psychiatry* 34 (Feb. 1995): 151–159.

Viogler, G. P., et al. "Influences of Genes and Shared Family Environment on Adult Body Mass Index Assessed in an Adoption Study by a Comprehensive Path Model." *International Journal of Obesity Related Metabolic Disorders* 19 (Jan. 1995): 40–45.

Wegar, Katarina. "Adoption and Mental Health: A Theoretical Critique of the Psychopathological Model." *American Journal of Orthopsychiatry* 65, no. 4 (1995): 540–548.

Winkler, Robin C., et al. *Clinical Practice in Adoption* (New York: Pergamon, 1988).

INDEX

ABOUT THE AUTHOR

Christine Adamec was born in Malden, Massachusetts. A "military brat," she had attended twelve schools including one in Izmir, Turkey, by the time she graduated from high school. She received her bachelor's degree in psychology from the University of New Hampshire and her master's in business administration from New Hampshire College.

After college graduation, Ms. Adamec received her commission as an Air Force officer and served on active duty. She was awarded the Air Force Commendation Medal for her service. Subsequently an Air Force Reservist, Ms. Adamec retired from the Air Force Reserve with the rank of major.

Ms. Adamec has been a professional writer since 1981, and has written hundreds of magazine features for such diverse publications as *McCall's, Employee Relations & Human Resources Bulletin, 80 Micro, Executive Female,* and *Expo Magazine.* She has also assisted many businesspeople, attorneys, and physicians with the editing and writing of articles, pamphlets, and books. The common denominator, says Adamec, is that everything she writes, no matter how brief or extensive, has the underlying goal of helping the reader in some way. Her self-help books include *There ARE Babies to Adopt* (updated for Kensington, 1996), *Start and Run a Profitable Freelance Writing Business* (Self-Counsel Press, 1994), and *How to Live with a Mentally Ill Person* (John Wiley & Sons, Inc., 1996).

She lives in Palm Bay, Florida, with her husband and their three children—an adopted son and a biological son and daughter.